The Pizza Tastes Great

Dialogues and Stories

William P. Pickett

Montclair State College
Passaic Adult Learning Center

PRENTICE HALL REGENTS, Englewood Cliffs, New Jersey 07632

Library of Congress Cataloging-in-Publication Data

PICKETT. WILLIAM P.
  The pizza tastes great.

  Includes index.
  1. English language—Text-books for foreign
speakers. 2. Readers—1950–   . I. Title.
PE1128.P483   1988   428.6'4   87-19142
ISBN 0-13-677626-4

Cover design: *Lundgren Graphics. Ltd.*
Manufacturing buyer: *Margaret Rizzi*
Illustrations by Marci Davis

To My Mother and Father

 ©1988 by Prentice Hall Regents
Prentice-Hall, Inc.
A Paramount Communications Company
Englewood Cliffs, New Jersey 07632

Printed in the United States of America
20 19 18 17

ISBN 0-13-677626-4

Prentice-Hall International (UK) Limited, *London*
Prentice-Hall of Australia Pty. Limited, *Sydney*
Prentice-Hall Canada Inc., *Toronto*
Prentice-Hall Hispanoamericana, S.A., *Mexico*
Prentice-Hall of India Private Limited, *New Delhi*
Prentice-Hall of Japan, Inc., *Tokyo*
Simon & Schuster Asia Pte. Ltd., *Singapore*
Editora Prentice-Hall do Brasil, Ltda., *Rio de Janeiro*

Contents

7 SPORTS AND FUN   127

8 SCHOOLS AND CHILDREN   148

Preface

Overview

The Pizza Tastes Great is a reader for beginners. Each chapter has four short dialogues and a story about the lives, problems, and hopes of ordinary people. The dialogues and stories are brief and interesting, control vocabulary and structures more than most beginning readers, and are written for and about adults. They will make a student's first steps in reading easy and enjoyable.

This book is written for college, community college, and high school students, as well as for adults who are studying at learning centers or on their own.

Objectives

The dialogues are meant to be listened to, read, and role played. No memorization is intended. The dialogues and stories never have a grammatical focus. They are written for the students to enjoy and comment on.

The Pizza Tastes Great aims to:

1. Improve listening comprehension
2. Provide reading material for beginning students
3. Increase students' basic vocabulary
4. Stimulate discussion
5. Improve pronunciation and intonation

Contents and Format

There are eight chapters in *The Pizza Tastes Great*. Each chapter has four dialogues of ten or eleven lines and a brief story that is divided into two parts. The words used in the dialogue or story are listed first.

In most of the dialogues, the speakers are given names used by both men and women, for example, Fran, Pat. In this way two men or two women can role play the characters in the dialogue as naturally as a man and a woman.

The dialogues and stories are followed by comprehension questions. In the first part of the book, all of these questions are factual. However, later in the book, the final comprehension question after most of the dialogues makes the students go beyond a literal interpretation of the text. Many of the final questions about the paragraphs of the stories do the same thing. These questions are marked with an asterisk (*) so the students will know that the answer cannot be found in the text.

After the comprehension questions, there is a section called *What About You?* This section fosters discussion and personal comments. *What About You?* is followed by a sentence completion exercise that tests and reinforces the vocabulary used in the dialogue or story.

After the dialogues, there is a final section which is either a modified cloze exercise, a word-grouping exercise, or a scrambled-sentence exercise. Each chapter closes with a vocabulary review exercise with synonyms and antonyms.

Working in Pairs

How teachers and students use the material in *The Pizza Tastes Great* will depend on their teaching and learning styles. However, the material lends itself to working in pairs. One way of doing this is to have the teacher read the words, short paragraph, and dialogue or story while the students listen. Then the class divides into pairs. The students ask each other the comprehension and discussion questions and do the vocabulary exercises together. The students then can go back to the beginning of the dialogue, read the vocabulary words and short paragraph, and role play the dialogue.

The Pizza Tastes Great and *The Chicken Smells Good*

The Pizza Tastes Great is written in a style and format similar to my earlier book *The Chicken Smells Good*. However, *The Pizza Tastes Great* is an easier book. Its dialogues and stories are shorter, its vocabulary and structures are more controlled, and its exercises are less difficult.

Answer Key and Audio Cassette

An answer key is provided at the back of the book so students can check their work.

An audio cassette of *The Pizza Tastes Great* is also available to facilitate use of the book in language labs, at home, and in the classroom.

Acknowledgments

I wish to thank the students and teachers of the Passaic Adult Learning Center and of Montclair State College for their help in field testing this book. I am also grateful to my wife, Dorothy, for her assistance in reviewing the text.

I also wish to thank everyone at Prentice Hall who assisted in publishing the book. I am especially grateful to Brenda White, the ESL editor, for her suggestions and enthusiasm.

1

Food

A Good Cook

Listen to and pronounce these words.

Nouns	Verbs	Contractions	Other
kitchen	cook	where is = where's	tired
living room	watch	what is = what's	good
wife	can	he is = he's	
dinner		she is = she's	
cook			
TV			

Mario is in the kitchen. He's cooking dinner. His wife is tired. She's watching TV in the living room.

Pat: Where's Mario?

Lynn: He's in the kitchen.

Pat: What's he doing?

Lynn: He's cooking dinner.

Pat: Where's his wife?

Lynn: In the living room.

Pat: What's she doing?

Lynn: Watching TV.

Pat: Can she cook?

Lynn: Yes, but she's tired, and he's a good cook.

I. Comprehension

Answer these questions about the dialogue.

1. Where's Mario?
2. What's he doing?
3. Where's his wife?
4. What's she doing?
5. Can she cook?
6. Why is Mario cooking?

II. Discussion: What About You?

Discuss these questions in pairs or small groups.

1. Can you cook?
2. Do you like to cook?
3. Are you a good cook?

III. Sentence Completion

Complete the sentences with these words.

cooking   **where's**   **dinner**   **watching**

1. Rita is _watching_ the children.
2. _____ my pen?
3. Sam is _____ spaghetti.
4. When are we going to eat _____ ?

tired   **wife**   **kitchen**   **can**

5. There's a clock in the _____ .
6. _____ Phil drive?
7. It's late and I'm _____ .
8. Ann isn't my sister; she's my _____ .

IV. Paragraph Completion

Complete the paragraphs with these words.

cooking   **kitchen**   **good**   **dinner**

Mario is in the _kitchen_ . It's time for _____
and he's _____ tonight. He's a _____ cook.

watching   **can**   **tired**   **wife**

Mario's _____ is in the living room. She
_____ cook, but she's _____ . She's
_____ TV.

We Eat a Lot

Listen to and pronounce these words.

Nouns	**Verbs**	**Contractions**	**Other**	
car	see	they are = they're	on top of	sure
key	eat	you are = you're	right	if
supermarket	want	I am = I'm	thanks	okay
package			where	busy
a lot			again	heavy

Terry is looking for her car keys. She's going to the supermarket. Chris isn't busy. He's going with her.

Terry: Did you see my car keys?

Chris: They're on top of the TV.

Terry: You're right. Thanks!

Chris: Where are you going?

Terry: To the supermarket.

Chris: Again?

Terry: Yes, we eat a lot.

Chris: Do you want me to go with you?

Terry: Sure, if you can.

Chris: Okay. I'm not busy.

Terry: Good. The packages will be heavy.

I. Comprehension

Answer these questions about the dialogue.

1. What is Terry looking for?
2. Where are the car keys?
3. Where is Terry going?
4. Does Terry want Chris to go to the supermarket too?
5. Does Chris have a lot to do?
6. Will the packages be light or heavy?

II. Discussion: What About You?

Discuss these questions in pairs or small groups.

1. Do you buy your food at a supermarket?
2. What's the name of the supermarket? Where is it?
3. Do you buy a lot of food at the supermarket?

III. Sentence Completion

Complete the sentences with these words.

> **on top of**   **if**   **again**   **key**

1. Come _____ , please.
2. _____ it's nice tomorrow, we'll go to the park.
3. Do you have the _____ to the house?
4. The box is _____ the cabinet.

> **package**   **a lot**   **heavy**   **busy**

5. Ed goes to the movies _____ .
6. What's in that _____ ?
7. Janet can't help you now. She's very _____ .
8. The table is _____ . It's not easy to move.

IV. Word Groups

Circle the three words that go together.

1. (yes)   (sure)   no   (okay)
2. eat   see   drink   cook
3. with   to   on top of keys
4. busy   bread   supermarket apples
5. do   will   right   did

A Little Milk but No Sugar

Listen to and pronounce these words.

Nouns	Verbs	Contractions	Other
cup	get	do not = don't	something
coffee	drink		little
tea	please		no
milk	keep		never
sugar	help		why
night	relax		awake
	like		

Carol gets Gerry a cup of coffee. Gerry likes a little milk in her coffee, but no sugar. Carol never drinks coffee at night. It keeps him awake.

Carol: Can I get you something to drink?

Gerry: A cup of coffee, please.

Carol: With milk and sugar?

Gerry: A little milk, but no sugar.

Carol: I never drink coffee at night.

Gerry: Why not?

Carol: It keeps me awake.

Gerry: What do you drink with dinner?

Carol: Tea, it helps me relax.

Gerry: I don't like tea.

I. Comprehension

Answer these questions about the dialogue.

1. What does Gerry want to drink?
2. Does Gerry want sugar?
3. Why doesn't Carol drink coffee at night?
4. What does Carol drink with dinner?
5. Why does Carol drink tea?
6. Does Gerry like tea?

II. Discussion: What About You?

Discuss these questions in pairs or small groups.

1. Do you drink coffee? A lot?
2. Do you drink tea? A lot?
3. Does coffee keep you awake?

III. Sentence Completion

Complete the sentences with these words.

at night   **never**   **please**   **something**

1. I'm hungry. I want _____ to eat.

2. My grandmother doesn't like to go out _____ .

3. _____ close the window.

4. Dan _____ gets sick.

little   **relax**   **awake**   **keep**

5. Is the baby _____ or is she sleeping?

6. Ruth likes a _____ salt on her food.

7. I want you to _____ your room clean.

8. After dinner, we watch TV and _____ .

IV. Paragraph Completion

Complete the paragraphs with these words.

please   **little**   **something**   **sugar**

Carol asks Gerry if she wants _____ to drink.

Gerry says, " _____ get me a cup of coffee with a

_____ milk, but no _____ ."

relax   **at night**   **awake**   **never**

Carol _____ drinks coffee _____ .

It keeps him _____ . He drinks tea. It helps him to

_____ .

A Big Menu

Listen to and pronounce these words.

Nouns	**Verbs**	**Contractions**		**Other**
menu	know	do not = don't	big	yesterday
turkey	have	I will = I'll	mashed	how about
peas	had =	I am = I'm	baked	perfect
potato	past of		very	any
fish	*have*			
roast beef				
vegetable				

Jackie and Fran are reading the menu at a restaurant. Jackie is going to have turkey. Fran decides to get roast beef.

Jackie: This is a big menu.

Fran: Yeah, what are you getting?

Jackie: Turkey, peas, and mashed potatoes.

Fran: I don't know what to get.

Jackie: They have very good fish.

Fran: No, I had fish yesterday.

Jackie: How about roast beef?

Fran: Perfect. I'll get roast beef and a baked potato.

Jackie: What vegetable are you getting?

Fran: I'm not getting any. I don't like vegetables.

I. Comprehension

Answer these questions about the dialogue.

1. Does the restaurant have a large menu?
2. What is Jackie getting to eat?
3. Is the fish at the restaurant good?
4. Why doesn't Fran want fish?
5. What is Fran getting?
6. Why isn't Fran getting a vegetable?

II. Discussion: What About You?

Discuss these questions in pairs or small groups.

1. Do you like to eat in restaurants?
2. What do you usually get when you go to a restaurant?
3. What vegetables do you like? What fruit do you like?

III. Sentence Completion

Complete the sentences with these words.

menu	**getting**	**perfect**	**vegetables**

1. I'm _____ a hamburger. What do you want?

2. This restaurant has a good _____ .

3. Peas and carrots are the only _____ John eats.

4. We love our new house. It's _____ for us.

fish	**any**	**how about**	**baked**

5. We're having hot dogs and _____ beans for supper.

6. Sonia likes turkey and chicken, but she doesn't like

   _____ .

7. _____ some cake?

8. We don't have _____ bread in the house.

IV. Word Groups

Circle the three words that go together.

1. roast beef	turkey	hamburger	steak
2. butter	milk	eggs	cream
3. banana	peas	lettuce	tomato
4. tea	soda	juice	sugar
5. menu	big	restaurant	food

The Pizza Tastes Great

Listen to and pronounce these words.

Nouns		**Verbs**	**Other**	
party	can	walk	married	everything
church	diet	talk	different	always
pizza	Coke	work	slow	favorite
ice cream	calorie	sit	slowly	only
pound	time	taste	fast	careful
weight		weigh	late	why
		think	early	so
			great	thin

Dave and Alice are married, but they're very different. Dave is slow. He walks, talks, and works slowly. He's late for everything. He's late for work, for parties, and for church. Alice is fast. She walks, talks, and works fast. She's early for everything. She's early for work, and she's early for parties and for church when she's not with Dave.

Dave is sitting in the living room. He's drinking a cold soda and eating pizza. The pizza tastes great. Dave is always eating something. Ice cream is his favorite food. He weighs two hundred and twenty pounds. He never thinks about his weight.

Alice is in the kitchen. She's drinking a can of diet Coke. It has only one calorie. Alice never eats cake or candy. Vegetables and fish are her favorite foods. Alice weighs a hundred and ten pounds. She thinks about her weight all the time, and she's careful about what she eats. That's why she's so thin.

I. Comprehension

Answer these questions about the story.

Paragraph 1

1. Is Dave fast or slow?
2. What is he late for?
3. Is Alice fast or slow?
4. When is she early for parties and for church?

Paragraph 2

1. Where is Dave?
2. What is he drinking? What is he eating?
3. What is his favorite food?
4. How much does he weigh?

Paragraph 3

1. Where is Alice?
2. What is she drinking?
3. What are her favorite foods?
4. How much does she weigh?

II. Discussion: What About You?

Discuss these questions in pairs or small groups.

1. Do you like to work slowly or fast?
2. Are you usually late or early for things?
3. Do you like fish?
4. Do you like ice cream? Cake? Candy?
5. What is your favorite food?
6. What are some favorite foods in your country?
7. How much do you weigh?

III. Sentence Completion

Complete the sentences with these words.

> **always**   **late**   **favorite**   **fast**

1. I'm going. I don't want to be _____ for school.
2. Pete _____ eats a big breakfast.
3. The train is going very _____ .
4. Baseball is my _____ sport.

> **slowly**   **weigh**   **early**   **diet**

5. Irene is going to bed _____ . She's tired.
6. How much does your son _____ ?
7. Bob is fat. That's why he's on a _____ .
8. Speak _____ . Anwar doesn't know much English.

> **pounds**   **so**   **only**   **careful**

9. It's _____ a block to the post office.
10. I'm going to the store to get milk and five _____ of sugar.
11. Be _____ with that knife!
12. It's _____ nice to be home.

> **living room**   **different**   **calories**   **thin**

13. I don't like my doctor. I'm going to go to a _____ one.
14. Florence wants to be _____ , but she loves to eat.
15. The cat is in the _____ .
16. Candy has a lot of _____ .

Alice Loves to Shop and Talk

Listen to and pronounce these words.

Nouns		Verbs		Other	
clothes	football	spend	say	happy	both
thing	basketball	save	fight	about	other
word	baseball	put	was = past	much	anything
phone	show	love	of *be*	few	alone
hour	music	shop	drive	friendly	because
program	news	buy	listen (to)	also	very
sport	in love			quiet	same
ball game				everyone	

Dave doesn't like to spend money. He likes to save it and put it in the bank. Alice loves to shop and spend money. She's always buying new clothes and things for the house. Dave isn't happy about this, but he doesn't say much. He doesn't like to fight with his wife.

Dave is a man of few words. He's friendly, but he's also quiet. No one knows what Dave is thinking. Everyone knows what Alice is thinking. She loves to talk. The other day she was on the phone for two hours.

Both Dave and Alice like to watch TV, but they like different programs. Dave likes sports. He watches football, basketball, and baseball games. Alice doesn't know anything about sports and never watches them on TV. She likes to watch movies and shows with music.

When Dave is driving alone, he listens to the news or a ball game. When Alice is driving alone, she listens to music. Dave and Alice are in love and very happy, but it's not because they're the same.

I. Comprehension

Answer these questions about the story.

Paragraph 1

1. What does Dave like to do with his money?
2. What does Alice like to buy?
3. Is Dave happy when she buys these things?
4. Does he like to fight with his wife?

Paragraph 2

1. Does Dave talk a lot?
2. Is he friendly?
3. Does Alice talk a lot?
4. How long was she on the phone the other day?

Paragraph 3

1. Do Dave and Alice like to watch the same TV programs?
2. What does he like to watch?
3. What does she like to watch?

Paragraph 4

1. What does Dave listen to when he's driving alone?
2. What does Alice listen to when she's driving alone?

II. Discussion: What About You?

Discuss these questions in pairs or small groups.

1. Do you like to shop?
2. Do you like to talk a lot?
3. Do you talk much on the phone?
4. Do you like to watch TV?
5. What programs do you watch?
6. Do you listen to the radio much?
7. What programs do you listen to?

III. Sentence Completion

Complete the sentences with these words.

> **clothes**   **spend**   **few**   **because**

1. I'm going to visit my brother for a _____ days.
2. Pat is washing the _____ .
3. Don can't go to the show _____ he's sick.
4. We have sixty dollars to _____ .

> **news**   **buying**   **also**   **about**

5. Abe is _____ flowers for his wife.
6. Nancy and Jim are talking _____ their daughter.
7. Judy is watching the _____ on TV.
8. Jessica likes to dance; she _____ likes to sing.

> **friendly**   **same**   **shop**   **listening**

9. The students are _____ to the teacher read a story.
10. Barbara will help us. She's _____ .
11. My sister and I _____ on Saturday afternoons.
12. Paul and Frank go to the _____ school.

> **save**   **fighting**   **alone**   **very**

13. You're going to need a hat. It's _____ cold.
14. No one is in the office with Ben. He's _____ .
15. I want to _____ a hundred dollars this month.
16. Joan and her husband are always _____ .

WORD REVIEW

Synonyms

Synonyms are words that have the same or similar meanings. Next to the sentences, write a synonym for the underlined word or words.

a lot	**can**	**great**	**little**

1. We have a small problem. *little* _____
2. Bill is able to swim. _____
3. Ghandi was a very good man. _____
4. I don't know much about Lisa. _____

few	**watching**	**dinner**	**also**

5. There are only a small number of fish in the river.

    _____

6. In the United States, most people eat their big meal at night.

    _____

7. Henry is looking at a football game. _____
8. Debbie is hungry and I am too. _____

Antonyms

Antonyms are words that have opposite meanings. In the blank spaces, write an antonym for each word.

on top of	**heavy**	**night**	**never**

1. day _night_____   3. always _____
2. under _____   4. light _____

fast	**hot**	**different**	**new**

5. old _____   7. slow _____
6. cold _____   8. same _____

2

Health

A Toothache

Listen to and pronounce these words.

Nouns	Verbs	Contractions	Other
time	go	it is = it's	two
o'clock	drive	I am = I'm	late
dentist	hear		there
tooth			sure
ache			very
toothache			bad
			sorry

Lee has a toothache. He's going to the dentist. It's two o'clock and he's late. Pat offers to drive him to the dentist.

Lee: What time is it?

Pat: It's two o'clock.

Lee: Oh no, I'm late!

Pat: Where are you going?

Lee: To the dentist.

Pat: Can I drive you there?

Lee: Sure! That will help.

Pat: Do you have a toothache?

Lee: Yes, and it's very bad.

Pat: I'm sorry to hear that.

I. Comprehension

Answer these questions about the dialogue.

1. What time is it?
2. Is Lee early or late?
3. Where is Lee going?
4. How is Pat going to help Lee?
5. Why is Lee going to the dentist?
6. Is Lee's toothache very bad?

II. Discussion: What About You?

Discuss these questions in pairs or small groups.

1. When was the last time you went to the dentist?
2. Do you go to the dentist often?
3. Do you like to go to the dentist?

III. Sentence Completion

Complete the sentences with these words.

time	sure	o'clock	there

1. You sit _____ and I'll sit here.
2. We can't stop now. We don't have _____ .
3. Jay goes to lunch at twelve _____ .
4. Can Dorothy cook? _____ she can.

toothache	very	sorry	hear

5. Allison is _____ thin.
6. I think I _____ someone at the door.
7. Brian has a _____ . He's going to call the dentist.
8. Dick is _____ that he can't go to the party.

IV. Paragraph Completion

Complete the paragraphs with these words.

late	time	there	o'clock

Lee asks Pat what _____ it is. Pat tells him it's two

_____ . Lee is going to the dentist, and he's

_____ . Pat offers to drive him _____ .

hears	toothache	sorry	very

Lee has a _____ and it's _____ bad.

When Pat _____ how bad it is, she says she's

_____ .

Sneezing a Lot

Listen to and pronounce these words.

Nouns	Verbs	Contractions	Other
God	bless	I am = I'm	so
cold	thank	that is = that's	better
winter	sneeze		soon
Contac	hope		every
	feel		sleepy
	take		

Carol is sneezing a lot. She has a cold. She's taking medicine that makes her sleepy.

Carol: Ah-choo!

Jamie: God bless you!

Carol: Thank you.

Jamie: Do you have a cold?

Carol: Yes, that's why I'm sneezing so much.

Jamie: I hope you feel better soon.

Carol: I get a bad cold every winter.

Jamie: Are you taking anything for your cold?

Carol: I'm taking Contac.

Jamie: Does it help?

Carol: Yes, but it makes me sleepy.

I. Comprehension

Answer these questions about the dialogue.

1. Why does Jamie say, "God bless you?"
2. What does Carol have?
3. Is Carol sneezing a lot?
4. What does Jamie hope?
5. What is Carol taking for her cold?
6. How does Contac make Carol feel?

II. Discussion: What About You?

Discuss these questions in pairs or small groups.

1. Do you get colds often?
2. What medicine do you take when you have a cold?
3. How much does the medicine help?

III. Sentence Completion

Complete the sentences with these words

> **feels**   **soon**   **sleepy**   **God**

1. You drive. I'm _____ .
2. Are we going to eat _____ ?
3. Thank _____ everyone is fine.
4. Jeff _____ tired. He had a busy week.

> **cold**   **better**   **hope**   **every**

5. Denise is a good cook, but her mother is _____ .
6. Eva writes to her sister _____ month.
7. The baby has a _____ , but he'll be okay.
8. We _____ you can come to the dance.

IV. Word Groups

Circle the three words that go together.

1. winter   January   spring   summer
2. doctor   dentist   teacher   nurse
3. feel   sleepy   tired   take
4. sneeze   much   cold   Contac
5. bless   love   help   buy

I Don't Feel Well

Listen to and pronounce these words.

Nouns	**Verbs**	**Contractions**	**Other**
jacket	look for	I am = I'm	well
doctor	feel	what is = what's	ten-thirty
problem		do not = don't	good-bye
fever		it is = it's	bye
pain			nothing
chest			serious
appointment			later

Lynn is looking for his jacket. He's going to the doctor. He doesn't feel well.

Chris: What are you looking for?

Lynn: My jacket. I'm going to the doctor.

Chris: Why? What's the problem?

Lynn: I'm not sure, but I don't feel well.

Chris: Do you have a fever?

Lynn: No, but I have a pain in my chest.

Chris: What time is your appointment?

Lynn: Ten-thirty. I'm going now. Bye.

Chris: Good-bye. I hope it's nothing serious.

Lynn: Thanks. See you later.

I. Comprehension

Answer these questions about the dialogue.

1. What is Lynn looking for?
2. Where is Lynn going?
3. Does Lynn have a fever?
4. What does Lynn have?
5. What time is Lynn's appointment?
6. What does Chris say to Lynn when Lynn is leaving?

II. Discussion: What About You?

Discuss these questions in pairs or small groups.

1. Do you have a doctor?
2. What's the doctor's name?
3. Does he know your first language?

III. Sentence Completion

Complete the sentences with these words.

> **looking for**   **pain**   **well**   **appointment**

1. Tony isn't _____ . He can't go to school today.
2. Betty is _____ a job.
3. When is your _____ with Mrs. Browski?
4. The _____ in my leg is bad.

> **nothing**   **serious**   **fever**   **later**

5. The accident is _____ ! Call the police!
6. Angela isn't in her office now. Can you call back
   _____ ?
7. Steve is hot. He has a _____ .
8. There is _____ in the desk.

IV. Paragraph Completion

Complete the paragraphs with these words.

> **well**   **looking for**   **pain**   **fever**

Lynn is _____ his jacket. He doesn't feel
_____ . He's going to the doctor. He doesn't have a
_____ , but he has a _____ in his chest.

> **nothing**   **serious**   **later**   **appointment**

Lynn has a ten-thirty _____ with the doctor. Lynn's
problem may be _____ , but he and Chris hope that it's
_____ . Lynn is going to see Chris _____
and tell her what the doctor says.

A Sore Throat

Listen to and pronounce these words.

Nouns	Verbs	Contractions	Other
throat	sound	I am = I'm	terrible
voice	should	I will = I'll	sore
honey	rest		hot
work	hurt		today
idea	stay		tomorrow
			better
			so

Fran has a sore throat. She's not going to work today. She's going to stay home and rest.

Sandy: You sound terrible.

Fran: I have a sore throat.

Sandy: You should rest your voice.

Fran: I know. It hurts when I talk.

Sandy: What are you taking for your throat?

Fran: Hot tea and honey.

Sandy: That should help. Are you going to work today?

Fran: No, I'm staying home.

Sandy: Good idea.

Fran: I'll feel better tomorrow.

Sandy: I hope so.

I. Comprehension

Answer these questions about the dialogue.

1. How does Fran sound?
2. What is Fran's problem?
3. What does Sandy say Fran should do?
4. What is Fran taking for her throat?
5. Is Fran going to work today?
6. Does Fran think she'll feel better tomorrow?

II. Discussion: What About You?

Discuss these questions in pairs or small groups.

1. Do you get a sore throat sometimes?
2. What do you take when you get a sore throat?
3. Does it help much?

III. Sentence Completion

Complete the sentences with these words.

terrible   **sore**   **voice**   **sounds**

1. Who is playing the piano? It _____ nice.

2. The fire was _____ .

3. My arm is _____ . I can't play baseball today.

4. Kathy sings well. She has a beautiful _____ .

should   **hurts**   **so**   **stay**

5. Is Ahmed going to the show? I think _____ .

6. _____ where you are! Don't move!

7. Jane's back _____ .

8. She _____ see a doctor.

IV. Word Groups

Circle the three words that go together.

1. today   tomorrow   always   yesterday
2. crackers   honey   sugar   candy
3. terrible   sound   bad   no good
4. hurt   sore   hot   pain
5. throat   neck   tongue   foot

A Doctor

Listen to and pronounce these words.

Nouns		**Verbs**		**Other**	
year	bill	live	marry	old	often
test	policeman	study	graduate	hard	a lot
boyfriend	department	stay up	(from)	smart	happy
salesman	store	have to	sell	last	easy
computer	daughter	wait	go out	medical	expensive
parent	college	finish	travel	single	another
		plan	pay	after	

Carmen is twenty-six years old, and she lives in Los Angeles, California. She is studying to be a doctor. It's hard, but she loves it. When she has a test, she stays up late and studies. Carmen is a very smart girl; you have to be smart to be a doctor. She's in her last year of medical school. She can't wait to finish.

Carmen is single, but she has a boyfriend. His name is Luis. Carmen and Luis plan to marry after she graduates from medical school. He's thirty and he's a salesman. He sells computers and makes good money. Luis and Carmen don't go out very often now. He has to travel a lot to sell computers, and she has to study.

Carmen's parents are from Mexico. They're very happy that she's in medical school, but it's not easy for them. It's expensive to go to medical school, and they're helping to pay the bills. Carmen's father is a policeman, and her mother works in a department store. They don't have much money. They also have another daughter, and she'll be going to college in two years.

I. Comprehension

Answer these questions about the story.

Paragraph 1

1. Where does Carmen live?
2. Does she like medical school?
3. What does Carmen do when she has a test?
4. In what year of medical school is she?

Paragraph 2

1. Is Carmen single or married?
2. When do she and Luis plan to marry?
3. What is Luis's job?
4. Why don't they go out often now?

Paragraph 3

1. Where are Carmen's parents from?
2. How do they feel about having a daughter in medical school?
3. Why is it difficult for them to have a daughter in medical school?
4. What does Carmen's father do?
5. What is her mother's job?

II. Discussion: What About You?

Discuss these questions in pairs or small groups.

1. What country are you from?
2. Do you like to study English?
3. Do you think English is easy or difficult?
4. Why are you studying English?
5. Are you studying any other subjects? What other subjects?
6. Are you working outside your home?
7. If you are working outside your home, what is your job?

III. Sentence Completion

Complete the sentences with these words.

salesman	**have to**	**smart**	**finish**

1. We _____ do the dishes.

2. The car _____ wants us to buy the car from him.

3. When are they going to _____ painting the house?

4. Linda is a very good student. She's _____ .

bill	**a lot**	**single**	**go out**

5. Ellen isn't _____ ; she has a husband and two children.

6. We have a big telephone _____ this month.

7. Joe can't _____ tonight. He has work to do.

8. Jennifer reads _____ .

department stores	**graduate**	**another**	**sell**

9. Edna and Larry want to _____ their house.

10. Can I have _____ hamburger, please?

11. The shopping center has three large _____ .

12. Ivan is going to _____ from high school in June.

travel	**expensive**	**marry**	**last**

13. Doris likes Fred, but she doesn't want to _____ him.

14. Those earrings are very nice. Are they _____ ?

15. December is the _____ month of the year.

16. I like to _____ and see new places.

She Wants to Be Herself

Listen to and pronounce these words.

Nouns		Verbs	Other	
high school	hobby	compare	third	large
people	country	ride	nice	still
bike =	world	belong	angry	born
bicycle	friend	collect	like	first
club	grandparent	buy	(preposition)	more
member	Mexico	know about	herself	than
ride	Mexico City	visit	active	young
mile	teacher	was = past	some	important
collection	Spanish	of *be*	sometimes	
stamp	language	learn		

Regina is Carmen's sister. She's in her third year of high school. She's quiet and very nice. Everyone likes her, but people often compare her to Carmen. This makes her angry. She doesn't want to be like her sister; she wants to be herself.

Regina is an active girl. She loves to swim, dance, and ride her bike. She belongs to a bicycle club, and on Saturdays the members go for long rides. Sometimes they ride a hundred miles in a day.

Regina also collects stamps. She has stamps from every country in the world. She buys some and gets others from friends who know about her hobby. She has a large collection of stamps from Mexico. Her grandparents still live in Mexico City, and she visits them in the summer.

Regina wants to be a Spanish teacher. She was born in California, but Spanish was her first language. She knows Spanish and English well. Some of her friends don't want her to be a teacher. They say that teachers don't make much money. She knows that, but she says that many things in life are more important than money. She wants to help young people learn. Nothing is more important than that.

I. Comprehension

Answer these questions about the story.

Paragraph 1

1. Does Regina talk a lot?
2. What do people do that makes her angry?
3. Why doesn't she want to be compared to her sister?

Paragraph 2

1. Name three things that Regina likes to do.
2. What club does she belong to?
3. How far do the members of the club sometimes ride?

Paragraph 3

1. What is Regina's hobby?
2. How does she get her stamps?
3. Where do her grandparents live?

Paragraph 4

1. What does Regina want to be?
2. Why don't some of her friends want her to be a teacher?
3. Why does she want to be a teacher?

II. Discussion: What About You?

Discuss these questions in pairs or small groups.

1. How many brothers do you have? How many sisters?
2. Do you have a bike? Do you ride it much?
3. Do you or did you ever collect stamps?
4. Can you bring to class some stamps from your country?
5. Do you have a hobby? If you do, what is it?
6. Are your grandparents still living? If they are, where do they live?
7. What things in life are more important than money?

III. Sentence Completion

Complete the sentences with these words.

> **compare**   **angry**   **like**   **herself**

1. Judy is looking at _____ in the mirror.
2. We should _____ the chairs before we buy one.
3. Eric talks and acts _____ his father.
4. The boss gets _____ when we're late for work.

> **ride**   **belongs**   **member**   **collect**

5. Is Gene a _____ of the basketball team?
6. This isn't my typewriter. It _____ to my friend.
7. When is the teacher going to _____ the books?
8. The children want to _____ on the train.

> **hobby**   **know about**   **collection**   **still**

9. The museum has a large _____ of art.
10. Is the soup _____ hot?
11. Gladys takes very good pictures. It's her _____ .
12. We didn't _____ your trip to Italy.

> **was**   **first**   **born**   **than**

13. George is working at a bank. It's his _____ job.
14. Kareem _____ happy to see us.
15. Cecilia is older _____ her brother.
16. Where were you _____ ?

WORD REVIEW

Synonyms

Synonyms are words that have the same or similar meanings. Next to the sentences, write a synonym for the underlined word or words.

| **terrible** | **stay** | **test** | **have to** |

1. Was the <u>exam</u> long? _____
2. Lauren has a <u>very bad</u> headache. _____
3. Garry and I <u>must</u> go now. _____
4. We can't <u>remain</u> here. _____

| **smart** | **rest** | **hard** | **finish** |

5. Did you <u>complete</u> your homework? _____
6. Rebecca is very <u>intelligent</u>. _____
7. I'm learning to ski, but it's <u>difficult</u>. _____
8. It was a busy day. We had no time to <u>relax</u>. _____

Antonyms

Antonyms are words that have opposite meanings. In the blank spaces, write an antonym for each word.

| **late** | **winter** | **bad** | **well** |

1. summer _____   3. early _____
2. sick _____   4. good _____

| **after** | **happy** | **last** | **better** |

5. first _____   7. worse _____
6. before _____   8. sad _____

3

Birthdays

Good News

Listen to and pronounce these words.

Nouns	**Verbs**	**Contractions**	**Other**
news	phone	that is = that's	great
beginning	say	when is = when's	so
December		I am = I'm	me too
			or
			due
			tonight
			hello

Kim is going to have a baby. She wants a girl. The baby is due in December.

Pat: I have some good news.
Terry: What is it?
Pat: Kim is going to have a baby.
Terry: That's great! I'm so happy for her.
Pat: Me too!
Terry: Do they want a boy or a girl?
Pat: A girl.
Terry: When's the baby due?
Pat: In the beginning of December.
Terry: I'm going to phone Kim tonight.
Pat: That's nice. Say hello for me.

I. Comprehension

Answer these questions about the dialogue.

1. What is the good news Pat has?
2. What does Terry say when she hears that Kim is going to have a baby?
3. Do Kim and her husband want a boy or a girl?
4. When does the doctor think the baby will be born?
5. Who is going to phone Kim tonight?
6. What does Pat ask Terry to say?

II. Discussion: What About You?

Discuss these questions in pairs or small groups.

1. Do you have any children?
2. If you do, how many do you have?
3. How many are boys? How many are girls?

III. Sentence Completion

Complete the sentences with these words.

> **news**   **great**   **phones**   **so**

1. Peggy _____ her mother every night.
2. Miss Fischer is a _____ nurse.
3. Your son is getting _____ big!
4. Did you hear the _____ about Bill?

> **beginning**   **or**   **due**   **me too**

5. I'm going to get a hot dog. _____ , I love hot dogs.
6. The _____ of the book is very good.
7. The train is _____ in five minutes.
8. Do you want coffee _____ tea?

IV. Paragraph Completion

Complete the paragraphs with these words.

> **too**   **great**   **news**   **so**

Pat has some good _____ . Kim is going to have a baby.
Pat tells Terry about the baby. Terry thinks that's _____ .
She's _____ happy for Kim. Pat is happy for her
_____ .

> **beginning**   **say**   **due**   **phone**

The baby is _____ in the _____ of
December. Terry is going to _____ Kim tonight. Pat
asks Terry to _____ hello for him.

Is She Pretty?

Listen to and pronounce these words.

Nouns	**Contractions**	**Other**
cousin	what is = what's	how
birthday	that is = that's	twenty-four
age	I am = I'm	pretty
	she is = she's	too
		single
		married
		too bad

Maria is Kathy's cousin and it's her birthday. Kathy is going to Maria's house after dinner. Maria is twenty-four. She's pretty and very nice.

Kathy: Today is my cousin's birthday.

Steve: What's your cousin's name?

Kathy: Maria. I'm going to her house after dinner.

Steve: How old is she?

Kathy: She's twenty-four.

Steve: Hmm. She's my age. Is she pretty?

Kathy: Yes, and she's very nice, too.

Steve: Is she single?

Kathy: No, she's married and has two children.

Steve: Oh, that's too bad!

I. Comprehension

Answer these questions about the dialogue.

1. Whose birthday is it?
2. Where is Kathy going after dinner?
3. How old is Maria?
4. Is she the same age as Steve?
5. Is she beautiful? Is she nice?
6. Why does Steve say it's too bad that she's married and has two children?

II. Discussion: What About You?

Discuss these questions in pairs or small groups.

1. Do you have any cousins?
2. How many cousins do you have?
3. Where do they live?

III. Sentence Completion

Complete the sentences with these words.

> **birthday**   **cousins**   **too**   **age**

1. Ken and I are going to the park. Do you want to go,

   _____ ?

2. We're going to have a _____ party for Mimi.

3. At what _____ do children start school?

4. My mother and his mother are sisters. We're _____ .

> **how**   **pretty**   **married**   **too bad**

5. Cindy has _____ eyes.

6. _____ big is the house?

7. It's _____ that it's raining.

8. Are Nick and Rose _____ ?

IV. Word Groups

Circle the three words that go together.

1. cousin   friend   uncle   brother

2. pretty   handsome   beautiful   nice

3. breakfast   coffee   lunch   dinner

4. single   party   gift   birthday

5. my   your   her   she's

A Cake

Listen to and pronounce these words.

Nouns	Verbs	Contractions	Other
bakery	there is	that is = that's	near
minute	get	do not = don't	here
cake	buy	she is = she's	there
bread	pay	I will = I'll	whose
			anything
			else
			back

Jackie is going to buy a birthday cake for his daughter. She's ten. Leslie asks Jackie to get some bread at the bakery.

Jackie: Is there a bakery near here?

Leslie: Yes, you can get there in five minutes.

Jackie: That's good. I don't have much time.

Leslie: Why are you going to the bakery?

Jackie: To buy a birthday cake.

Leslie: Whose birthday is it?

Jackie: My daughter's. She's ten.

Leslie: That's nice. Will you get some bread for me?

Jackie: Sure, do you want anything else?

Leslie: No thanks. I'll pay you when you get back.

I. Comprehension

Answer these questions about the dialogue.

1. How long will it take to get to the bakery?
2. Why is Jackie going to the bakery?
3. Whose birthday is it?
4. How old is Jackie's daughter?
5. What is Jackie going to get for Leslie?
6. When is Leslie going to pay Jackie?

II. Discussion: What About You?

Discuss these questions in pairs or small groups.

1. Is there a bakery near your home?
2. Do you go to a bakery much?
3. What do you buy at the bakery?

III. Sentence Completion

Complete the sentences with these words.

bakery	**near**	**is there**	**anything**

1. I don't have _____ to do now.

2. Amy lives _____ me.

3. _____ a radio in your room?

4. That _____ has very good cookies and pies.

get	**whose**	**pay**	**else**

5. _____ pen is this?

6. What _____ do we need?

7. Ron wants to _____ to work early.

8. How much do I have to _____ for the tickets to the show?

IV. Paragraph Completion

Complete the paragraphs with these words.

bakery	**near**	**daughter**	**there is**

Jackie wants to buy a birthday cake for his _____ .
He's going to a _____ to get the cake. Leslie tells him
_____ one _____ her house.

gets back	**time**	**pay**	**else**

Jackie can get there in five minutes. He's happy about that because
he doesn't have much _____ . Leslie asks him to get some
bread for her. She doesn't want anything _____ . She is
going to _____ Jackie when he _____ .

A Birthday Present

Listen to and pronounce these words.

Nouns	Verbs	Contractions	Other
shirt	get	do not = don't	yet
briefcase	got = past of *get*	did not = didn't	different
idea	let	that is = that's	how about
	use	it is = it's	one
		he will = he'll	of course

Jamie is getting a birthday present for Ted. Last year she got him a shirt. She wants to get him something different this year.

Chris: What are you getting Ted for his birthday?
Jamie: I don't know yet.
Chris: You can always get him a shirt.
Jamie: But I got him one last year.
Chris: Oh, that's right. Let me think.
Jamie: I want to get him something different.
Chris: How about a briefcase?
Jamie: Good idea! His briefcase is getting old.
Chris: And it's something he'll use every day.
Jamie: Of course! Why didn't I think of that?

I. Comprehension

Answer these questions about the dialogue.

1. Why is Jamie getting a gift for Ted?
2. Does Jamie know what to get him?
3. What did Jamie get him last year?
4. What does Jamie think of getting him a briefcase?
5. What's the problem with the briefcase he has?
6. Will he use the briefcase a lot?

II. Discussion: What About You?

Discuss these questions in pairs or small groups.

1. When is your birthday?
2. Do you do anything special on your birthday?
3. Do they celebrate birthdays in a different way in your country?

III. Sentence Completion

Complete the sentences with these words.

briefcase	**got**	**yet**	**of course**

1. _____ Sally is going to the dance. She loves to dance.

2. The letter is in my _____ .

3. It isn't snowing _____ .

4. Mark _____ a new stereo yesterday. He likes to listen to music.

let	**different**	**one**	**how about**

5. Do you want a small box of candy or a large _____ ?

6. I'll _____ you use my car.

7. _____ some ice cream?

8. We're taking a _____ road home.

IV. Word Groups

Circle the three words that go together.

1. of course   clearly   why   sure

2. write   know   understand   think

3. shirt   tie   shoes   jacket

4. month   week   afternoon   year

5. store   briefcase   notebook   pen

Forty and Getting Gray

Listen to and pronounce these words.

Nouns		Verbs	Other	
godfather	job	relax	long	last
fire	life	get	gray	brave
firehouse	sofa	save	still	large
firefighter	insurance	act	young	well
hair	company	play	every	interesting
tennis	computer	jog	strong	
salary		pay attention (to)		

It's nine o'clock at night, and Tom is relaxing. He's watching an old movie on TV. The name of the movie is *The Godfather*. It's a long movie and very good.

Tom is a firefighter. His salary isn't great, but he loves his job. He likes to help people and he's strong. Last year he saved a woman's life. Her house was on fire. Tom is brave.

Today is Tom's birthday. He's forty. They had a big party for him at the firehouse. Tom's hair is getting gray, but he still feels and acts young. He plays tennis every week and jogs a lot.

Gloria is Tom's wife, and she's sitting on the sofa. She's reading a book. She's not paying any attention to *The Godfather*. Gloria loves to read. When she's reading, she doesn't think of anything else.

Gloria works for a large insurance company. She works with computers. Her job pays well and it's very interesting. Gloria knows a lot about computers and likes to work with them.

I. Comprehension

Answer these questions about the story.

Paragraph 1

1. What is Tom doing?
2. What movie is he watching?

Paragraph 2

1. What is Tom's job? Does he like it?
2. What did he do last year that was special?

Paragraph 3

1. How old is Tom?
2. What did they have for him at the firehouse?

Paragraph 4

1. Who is sitting on the sofa?
2. What is she doing? Does she like to read?
3. Is she paying attention to *The Godfather?*

Paragraph 5

1. For whom does Gloria work?
2. What does she work with?
3. Does she get a good salary?

II. Discussion: What About You?

Discuss these questions in pairs or small groups.

1. Did you ever see *The Godfather?*
2. Did you like it?
3. Do you play tennis? Do you play often?
4. Do you jog? Do you jog often?
5. Do you read much?
6. What do you like to read?
7. Did you ever use a computer? Do you use one now?

III. Sentence Completion

Complete the sentences with these words.

relax	every	well	getting

1. Helen works _____ with Karl.

2. Edna goes to church _____ Sunday.

3. Alex is _____ fat.

4. I want to go home, sit down, and _____ .

last	on fire	still	brave

5. The building is _____ ! Don't use the elevator!

6. A good police officer must be _____ .

7. I visited my aunt and uncle _____ week.

8. Is the store _____ open?

feel	strong	jog	computers

9. Julia likes to _____ in the park.

10. I was sick yesterday, but I _____ fine today.

11. Many schools teach their students how to use _____ .

12. Garry is a football player and he's _____ .

pay attention	insurance	save	interesting

13. San Francisco is a very _____ city.

14. I have some life _____ , but I need more.

15. Everything is expensive today. It's not easy to _____ money.

16. _____ to the teacher!

On the Phone Too Much

Listen to and pronounce these words.

Nouns		Verbs	Other
telephone	magazine	ring	second
phone	interest	answer	usually
girlfriend	player	change	probably
math =	foot (singular)	stop	difficult
mathematics	feet (plural)	pass	hard
science	inch		favorite
subject	team		all right
chemist			tall
record			best

Gloria and Tom have two children, Dianne and Frank. Dianne is fifteen, and she's in her second year of high school. She's talking on the telephone to her girlfriend Joan. They talk a lot on the phone. When the phone rings, Dianne usually answers it. She knows it's probably for her. Tom and Gloria think Dianne is on the phone too much. They talk to her about the problem, but it's going to be difficult for her to change.

Dianne studies hard and does well in school. Math and science are her favorite subjects. She wants to go to college and study to be a chemist. She has a math test tomorrow. She's going to study for it when she stops talking to Joan.

Frank is in his room listening to records and reading a sports magazine. He's seventeen, and he's in his last year of high school. He'll graduate in June. Frank does all right in school. He passes all his subjects, but he doesn't like to study. His big interests are basketball, music, and his girlfriend. He's six feet three inches tall and is the best basketball player on the high school team. He hopes to play basketball in college.

I. Comprehension

Answer these questions about the story.

Paragraph 1

1. In what year of high school is Dianne?
2. What is she doing?
3. Do Dianne and Joan talk a lot on the phone?
4. When the phone rings, who usually answers it? Why?

Paragraph 2

1. Is Dianne a good student?
2. What are her favorite subjects?
3. What does she want to be?
4. What is she going to do when she stops talking to Joan?

Paragraph 3

1. What is Frank doing?
2. When is he going to graduate from high school?
3. What are his big interests?
4. How tall is he?

II. Discussion: What About You?

Discuss these questions in pairs or small groups.

1. Does anyone in your home talk a lot on the phone? Who?
2. When the phone rings in your home, who usually answers it? Why?
3. What are or were your favorite subjects in school?
4. Do you like math?
5. What magazines do you read?
6. Is basketball a popular sport in your country?
7. How tall are you?

III. Sentence Completion

Complete the sentences with these words.

usually   **subject**   **all right**   **change**

1. Kevin always does things in the same way. He doesn't like to

   _____ .

2. After dinner, I _____ take the dog for a walk.

3. Are you _____ ?

4. History is an interesting _____ .

answer   **best**   **hope**   **probably**

5. I _____ the bus comes soon.

6. Tania is the _____ student in the class.

7. We'll _____ go to the movies tonight.

8. You didn't _____ my question.

inches   **passed**   **favorite**   **hard**

9. The test wasn't easy, but I _____ it.

10. Roger works _____ .

11. There are twelve _____ in a foot.

12. Coffee is Debbie's _____ drink.

magazine   **second**   **interests**   **ringing**

13. This is our _____ trip to Disney World.

14. I'm going to buy a _____ to read on the train.

15. The bell is _____ .

16. What do you like to do? What are your _____ ?

WORD REVIEW

Synonyms

Synonyms *are words that have the same or similar meanings. Next to the sentences, write a synonym for the underlined word or words.*

pretty	**all right**	**phone**	**big**

1. Call me when you get home. _____

2. The flowers are beautiful. _____

3. London is a large city. _____

4. Is everything okay? _____

job	**so**	**children**	**of course**

5. This room is very hot. _____

6. Sal is a carpenter, and he likes his work. _____

7. Naturally it's cold in the winter. _____

8. How are the kids? _____

Antonyms

Antonyms *are words that have opposite meanings. In the blank spaces, write an antonym for each word.*

beginning	**married**	**buy**	**young**

1. sell _____   3. single _____

2. old _____   4. end _____

long	**play**	**large**	**stop**

5. go _____   7. small _____

6. short _____   8. work _____

4

Cars and Planes

Washing the Car

Listen to and pronounce these words.

Nouns	Verbs	Contractions	Other
care	wash	where is = where's	in front of
order	clean	what is = what's	again
mess	take care of	he is = he's	never
		it is = it's	always
		you are = you're	dirty

Don is washing his car. He washes his car a lot, but he never cleans his room. It's always dirty.

Carol: Where's Don?

Fran: He's in front of the house.

Carol: What's he doing?

Fran: Washing his car.

Carol: Not again?

Fran: Yes, he takes good care of his car.

Carol: But he never cleans his room.

Fran: I know. It's always dirty.

Carol: And nothing is in order.

Fran: You're right. His room is a mess.

I. Comprehension

Answer these questions about the dialogue.

1. Where's Don?
2. What's he doing?
3. Does he wash his car often?
4. Is his room clean?
5. How often does he clean his room?
6. Is anything in order in his room?

II. Discussion: What About You?

Discuss these questions in pairs or small groups.

1. Are you good at keeping your house or room clean and in order?
2. Do you know anyone like Don?
3. Do you have a car? Do you wash it yourself or do you take it to a car wash?

III. Sentence Completion

Complete the sentences with these words.

in order	**mess**	**in front of**	**always**

1. We _____ eat out on Saturday night.
2. Henry's desk is a _____ .
3. He should put his papers _____ .
4. Shirley sits _____ me in science class.

take care of	**again**	**dirty**	**never**

5. These clothes are _____ . I have to wash them.
6. The baby is crying _____ .
7. Herb smokes a lot, but he _____ drinks.
8. _____ your little brother. I'm going to the store.

IV. Paragraph Completion

Complete the paragraphs with these words.

takes	**in front of**	**care**	**washing**

Don is _____ his house. He's _____ his car. He _____ good _____ of his car, but not of his room.

in order	**mess**	**always**	**cleans**

Don never _____ his room. It's _____ dirty. Nothing in his room is _____ . It's a _____ .

Don't Worry

Listen to and pronounce these words.

Nouns	Verbs	Contractions	Other
officer	try	I will = I'll	how
coat hanger	get into	what is = what's	kind
police car	worry	can not = can't	
	open	do not = don't	
	wait	they are = they're	
		it is = it's	
		you are = you're	
		there is = there's	

Pat can't get into her car. She asks Chris, a police officer, to help. Chris says he can open her car with a coat hanger.

Pat: Can you help me, officer?

Chris: I'll try. What's the problem?

Pat: I can't get into my car.

Chris: Where are your keys?

Pat: They're in the car.

Chris: Don't worry. I can open it.

Pat: How can you do that?

Chris: With a coat hanger. It's easy.

Pat: Where can we get a coat hanger?

Chris: There's one in the police car. Wait here.

Pat: Thanks a lot! You're very kind.

I. Comprehension

Answer these questions about the dialogue.

1. What is Pat's problem?
2. Where are Pat's keys?
3. Who helps Pat?
4. What is Chris going to use to open the car?
5. Will it be difficult for Chris to open the car?
6. Where is Chris going to get a coat hanger?

II. Discussion: What About You?

Discuss these questions in pairs or small groups.

1. Did you ever lock your car keys in your car?
2. Were you able to open the car or did someone have to help you?
3. How did you or the other person open the car? Was it easy?

III. Sentence Completion

Complete the sentences with these words.

officer	**thanks**	**try**	**kind**

1. _____ for the gift! It's very nice.
2. Lucy is always helping someone. She's _____ .
3. Why did you stop our car, _____ ?
4. I'm not sure I can go to the dance, but I'll _____ .

there is	**hanger**	**worry**	**wait**

5. _____ for us! We want to go with you.
6. _____ a big dog in the yard.
7. My wife isn't well. I _____ about her.
8. Jack is putting his shirt on a _____ .

IV. Word Groups

Circle the three words that go together.

1. officer   policeman   firefighter   cop
2. rich   friendly   good   kind
3. truck   car   taxi   boat
4. what   there   where   how
5. hanger   sweater   key   coat

A Car Loan

Listen to and pronounce these words.

Nouns	Verbs	Contractions	Other
bank	cash	I will = I'll	wrong
check	apply (for)	I am = I'm	how much
loan	have to	it is = it's	about
	cost	will not = won't	thousand
		what is = what's	wow
		that is = that's	a lot of
			why

Sandy is going to the bank to apply for a loan. She has to buy a new car. Her car is ten years old.

Sandy: I want to go to the bank this afternoon.

Lee: I'll drive you there. I have to cash my check.

Sandy: Thanks. I'm going to apply for a loan.

Lee: Why do you need a loan?

Sandy: I have to buy a new car.

Lee: What's wrong with your car?

Sandy: It won't start and it's ten years old.

Lee: How much will a new car cost?

Sandy: About fifteen thousand dollars.

Lee: Wow! That's a lot of money.

Sandy: I know. That's why I need a loan.

I. Comprehension

Answer these questions about the dialogue.

1. Where is Sandy going?
2. Why is Lee going to the bank?
3. Why is Sandy going to the bank?
4. Why does Sandy need a loan?
5. What's wrong with Sandy's car?
6. How much will Sandy's car cost?

II. Discussion: What About You?

Discuss these questions in pairs or small groups.

1. Did you ever buy a new car? A used car?
2. How much did it cost?
3. Did you get a loan to buy it?

III. Sentence Completion

Complete the sentences with these words.

loan	a lot of	wrong	apply

1. There's something _____ with this telephone.

2. Mohammed needs a thousand dollars. He's going to ask his brother
   for a _____ .

3. Are you going to _____ for that job?

4. Michelle eats _____ candy.

cost	cash	have to	about

5. This is a big check. I hope the bank will _____ it.

6. There are _____ sixty rooms in the motel.

7. I _____ get my medicine at the drugstore.

8. What do these pants _____ ?

IV. Paragraph Completion

Complete the paragraphs with these words.

apply	buy	driving	loan

Lee is _____ Sandy to the bank. Sandy is going to the

bank to _____ for a _____ . She's going to

_____ a new car.

has to	wrong	a lot of	about

Sandy's car is ten years old, and there are many things

_____ with it. That's why she _____ get a

new one. Her new car is going to cost _____ fifteen thou-

sand dollars. That's _____ money.

Afraid of Flying

Listen to and pronounce these words.

Nouns	**Verbs**	**Contractions**	**Other**
meeting	feel	I am = I'm	comfortable
plane	understand	it is = it's	afraid (of)
flying		that is = that's	foolish
way		do not = don't	safe
			maybe

Lynn is going to a meeting in Dallas, Texas. She's flying there. She likes to fly, but her friend Terry is afraid of flying.

Terry: Where is your meeting?
Lynn: In Dallas, Texas.
Terry: How are you going?
Lynn: By plane.
Terry: Do you like to fly?
Lynn: Sure. It's fast and comfortable.
Terry: I'm afraid of flying.
Lynn: That's foolish. Flying is very safe.
Terry: Maybe, but I don't feel safe in a plane.
Lynn: I understand. A lot of people feel that way.

I. Comprehension

Answer these questions about the dialogue.

1. Where is Lynn's meeting?
2. How is Lynn going to the meeting?
3. Does Lynn like to fly?
4. Does Terry like to fly?
5. Why does Lynn like to fly?
6. Why doesn't Terry like to fly?

II. Discussion: What About You?

Discuss these questions in pairs or small groups.

1. Are you afraid of flying?
2. Do you fly much?
3. When you fly, where do you fly? Why?

III. Sentence Completion

Complete the sentences with these words.

safe   **understand**   **meeting**   **afraid**

1. Everyone is _____ of the boss.

2. Does Andy _____ what we want him to do?

3. Small cars don't use much gas, but I don't think they're

   _____ .

4. We have an important _____ tomorrow morning.

comfortable   **maybe**   **foolish**   **flying**

5. _____ Bert can help us.

6. Lilian is _____ to Paris tonight.

7. I like this chair. It's _____ .

8. It's snowing very hard. You're _____ to go out.

IV. Word Groups

Circle the three words that go together.

1. airport   fly   run   plane

2. foolish   stupid   crazy   afraid

3. men   money   people   women

4. Pennsylvania   Dallas   Saint Louis   Boston

5. meeting   appointment   chair   time

Two Boyfriends

Listen to and pronounce these words.

Nouns		Verbs	Other	
secretary	mechanic	answer	busy	poor
lawyer	dance	file	many	either
worker	dancer	type	excellent	however
mistake	fun	dance	handsome	certainly
restaurant	truth	fix	rich	fair
papers		tell (the truth)		
		hurt		

Linda is a secretary for a busy lawyer. She likes her job and is a good worker. She answers the phone, files papers, and types. She types well. She doesn't make many mistakes, and she's fast.

Linda is twenty-four years old, and she's single. She's a pretty girl, and she likes to dance. She also likes to eat in nice restaurants. Linda has two boyfriends, Mike and Ray.

Mike is a mechanic; he fixes cars. He's twenty-four and he's single. He likes to dance, and he's an excellent dancer. Every Saturday night he takes Linda to a dance. He loves Linda and wants to marry her. He doesn't know anything about Ray.

Linda has a lot of fun dancing with Mike, and she likes him very much. He's handsome and kind. He isn't rich, but he isn't poor either. Mechanics make good money. However, there's a big problem. Linda doesn't love Mike. He's only a good friend. She certainly doesn't want to marry him. She'll have to tell him the truth soon. She knows it's going to hurt him, but it's not fair to let him think she loves him.

I. Comprehension

Answer these questions about the story.

Paragraph 1

1. What is Linda's job?
2. What does she do at work?
3. Does she type well?

Paragraph 2

1. Is Linda single or married?
2. What two things does she like to do?

Paragraph 3

1. What is Mike's job?
2 Is he the same age as Linda?
3. Where does he take Linda every Saturday night?
4. What does he know about Ray?

Paragraph 4

1. Does Linda like Mike a lot?
2. Does she want to marry him? Why not?
3. When is she going to tell him the truth?

II. Discussion: What About You?

Discuss these questions in pairs or small groups.

1. Do you like your job?
2. Can you type? Can you type well?
3. Do you like to dance?
4. What is your favorite dance? What are the favorite dances in your country?
5. Are you a good dancer?
6. Do you go dancing often? Where?
7. Do you think that a couple who are going to marry should be about the same age?

III. Sentence Completion

Complete the sentences with these words.

busy	lawyer	file	mistakes

1. There are some _____ on this page. I'm going to type it again.

2. Scott isn't _____ now. He can see you.

3. This is an important letter. Please _____ it.

4. We're buying a house; we'll need a _____ .

however	excellent	hurt	either

5. Kay doesn't drive and I don't _____ .

6. Emily is an _____ doctor.

7. It's going to _____ Ted when I tell him he didn't get the job.

8. This cake is very good. _____ , I can't eat anymore.

answer	mechanic	fun	soon

9. We're having a lot of problems with our car. We need a good

   _____ .

10. The children are playing in the park. They're having

   _____ .

11. I have to _____ Martha's letter.

12. It's getting colder. Winter will be here _____ .

truth	fair	also	fix

13. Can you help me _____ this table?

14. You cook today and I'll cook tomorrow. That's _____ .

15. Ralph works eight hours a day, and he _____ goes to school at night.

16. Tell me the _____ . Do you like my new dress?

Will Linda Say Yes?

Listen to and pronounce these words.

Nouns		Verbs	Other	
driver	appetite	eat out	difficult	handsome
bus driver	walk	ask	heavy	favorite
salary	life (singular)		wild	of course
passenger	lives (plural)		polite	nervous
traffic	hope		usually	
snow	future			
wind	time			

Ray is twenty-six and he's single. He's a bus driver in Chicago. His salary is good, but he has a difficult job. Traffic is heavy in Chicago. Snow, wind, and wild drivers are also a problem. Ray tries to be polite to all the passengers, but that's not easy. Some of them aren't very polite to him.

Ray doesn't like to dance, but he loves to eat out. He's a big man and has a good appetite. Every Sunday he takes Linda to a nice restaurant. After dinner, they usually go for a long walk. They talk about their lives and hopes for the future. When the weather is bad, they go to a movie. Ray loves Linda very much and wants to marry her. He doesn't know anything about Mike.

Linda loves Ray a lot. She thinks about him all the time. He isn't handsome, and he doesn't have much money in the bank. However, he understands Linda and she understands him. This Sunday Ray is taking Linda to their favorite restaurant. He's going to ask her to marry him. Of course, he's a little nervous. Will she say yes? What do you think she'll say?

I. Comprehension

Answer these questions about the story.

Paragraph 1

1. What is Ray's job? Where does he work?
2. Why is his job difficult?
3. Does he try to be nice to all the passengers? Are all of them nice to him?

Paragraph 2

1. Where does Ray take Linda every Sunday?
2. What do they usually do after dinner?
3. What do they talk about?
4. Does Ray love Linda a lot?

Paragraph 3

1. What shows that Linda loves Ray?
2. Is he handsome? Is he rich?
3. Where are Ray and Linda going this Sunday?
4. What is he going to ask her?
5. Do you think she will say yes? Give a reason for your answer.

II. Discussion: What About You?

Discuss these questions in pairs or small groups.

1. Do you have a difficult job?
2. Are you a wild driver or a careful one?
3. Are you polite? Always? Usually?
4. Do you have a good appetite?
5. Do you eat out much?
6. Do you have a favorite restaurant? Where is it? What's its name?
7. Do you like to go for walks? Do you walk a lot?

III. Sentence Completion

Complete the sentences with these words.

salary   **heavy**   **wind**   **passengers**

1. Take an umbrella. We're going to get _____ rain.

2. How many _____ are on the plane?

3. Virginia is the president of the company, and she gets a big

   _____ .

4. The _____ is cold. You'll need a coat.

traffic   **eat out**   **future**   **polite**

5. We don't know what the _____ will bring.

6. I go to work early when there isn't much _____ .

7. When Len wants something, he always says "please." He's

   _____ .

8. It's nice to _____ , but it's expensive.

difficult   **hopes**   **wild**   **appetite**

9. Our business is doing well, and we have _____ it'll do better.

10. Marilyn loves to eat. She has a big _____ .

11. Is it _____ to use that computer?

12. Leo has some _____ ideas. I don't pay attention to them.

nervous   **of course**   **handsome**   **usually**

13. Most of the girls like Alan. He's friendly and very

    _____ .

14. _____ money is important.

15. Sara _____ has a sandwich and tea for lunch.

16. I get _____ when I take a test.

WORD REVIEW

Synonyms

Synonyms *are words that have the same or similar meanings. Next to the sentences, write a synonym for the underlined word or words.*

excellent	**foolish**	**many**	**right**

1. There are <u>a large number of</u> tall buildings in New York City.

   _____

2. I hope you're <u>correct</u>. _____

3. This camera is <u>very good</u>. _____

4. It's <u>stupid</u> to smoke, but it's hard to stop. _____

mistake	**kind**	**handsome**	**however**

5. It was <u>nice</u> of you to visit me in the hospital. _____

6. It's a sunny day. <u>But</u> it's cold. _____

7. There's a big <u>error</u> in this bill. _____

8. Nicole wants a husband who is rich and <u>good looking</u>.

   _____

Antonyms

Antonyms *are words that have opposite meanings. In the blank spaces, write an antonym for each word.*

nothing	**dirty**	**open**	**easy**

1. close _____   3. difficult _____

2. everything _____   4. clean _____

many	**rich**	**future**	**truth**

5. poor _____   7. few _____

6. lie _____   8. past _____

5

Work and Shopping

On Sale

Listen to and pronounce these words.

Nouns	**Verbs**	**Contractions**	**Other**
price	look	I am = I'm	terrific
sale	was = past of *be*	that is = that's	glad
Sears	shop		how much
			too

Fran thinks Lee's new coat looks terrific. It was on sale for eighty dollars at Sears.

Lee: Do you like my new coat?

Fran: It looks terrific!

Lee: I'm glad you like it.

Fran: How much was it?

Lee: Eighty dollars.

Fran: That's a good price.

Lee: Yeah, it was on sale.

Fran: Where did you get it?

Lee: At Sears.

Fran: I like to shop there, too.

I. Comprehension

Answer these questions about the dialogue.

1. What does Fran say about Lee's new coat?
2. Is Lee happy that Fran likes her coat?
3. How much was the coat?
4. Was that a good price?
5. Why was the price low?
6. Where did Lee get the coat?
*7. Why do you think Fran also likes to shop at Sears?

II. Discussion: What About You?

Discuss these questions in pairs or small groups.

1. Where do you shop for clothes?
2. Do you usually wait for sales to buy clothes?
3. Do you ever shop at Sears? Do you ever use the Sears Catalog to shop?

*Questions with an asterisk (*) do not have answers in the dialogues or stories.

III. Sentence Completion

Complete the sentences with these words.

> **glad**   **looks**   **price**   **on sale**

1. What's the _____ of this sofa?
2. I'm _____ to see you again.
3. These shirts are _____ . They're only nine dollars.
4. Al _____ good.

> **terrific**   **how much**   **too**   **shopping**

5. Brenda isn't home. She's _____ .
6. _____ is that tape recorder?
7. It was a _____ party. Everyone had a good time.
8. Pamela wants to be a nurse, and I do _____ .

IV. Paragraph Completion

Complete the paragraphs with these words.

> **glad**   **looks**   **how much**   **terrific**

Lee buys a new coat. She asks Fran how it _____ . He
says that it's _____ . She's _____ that he
likes it. He asks her _____ it was.

> **too**   **price**   **shop**   **on sale**

The coat was eighty dollars. The _____ was good
because it was _____ . Lee got the coat at Sears. She
likes to _____ there, and Fran does _____ .

A New Dress

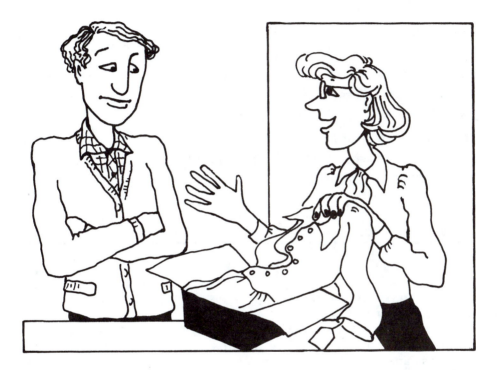

Listen to and pronounce these words.

Nouns	Verbs	Contractions	Other
dear	let	it is = it's	who
honey	get	do not = don't	full (of)
closet		what is = what's	one
style		they are = they're	wrong

Janet buys a new dress. Her husband, Kevin, can't understand why she needs a new dress. She has a closet full of them.

Kevin: Who is it?

Janet: It's me, dear.

Kevin: Don't you have your key?

Janet: No, let me in!

Kevin: What's in that box? What did you get?

Janet: A new dress, honey.

Kevin: But you have a closet full of dresses.

Janet: I know, but I need a new one.

Kevin: What's wrong with all the other dresses?

Janet: They're not in style.

I. Comprehension

Answer these questions about the dialogue.

1. Why can't Janet get in?
2. Who lets her in?
3. What does she have in the box?
4. Is Kevin happy about the new dress?
5. Does Janet have a lot of dresses?
6. What's the problem with the dresses she has?
*7. Why do you think dressmakers change styles so often?

II. Discussion: What About You?

Discuss these questions in pairs or small groups.

1. Do you like to buy new clothes?
2. Do you buy new clothes often?
3. Do you keep clothes that you're not using and will probably not use again?

III. Sentence Completion

Complete the sentences with these words.

dear	let	full of	wrong

1. _____ Grace look at the pictures.

2. I'll be there in a minute, _____ .

3. What's _____ with the elevator? Why isn't it running?

4. The cabinet in the classroom is _____ books.

closets	get	one	in style

5. Walter is going to _____ a new suit.

6. Are shorts skirts _____ ?

7. The bedroom has two _____ .

8. Are we going to take our new car or our old _____ ?

IV. Word Order

Make sentences of these words by putting them in the right order.

1. have / you / key / don't / your / ?
   <u>Don't you have your key?</u>

2. a closet / have / dresses / you / full of

   _____

3. dressses / wrong / the / all / what's / with / other / ?

   _____

4. not / style / they're / in

   _____

A Cashier

Listen to and pronounce these words.

Nouns	Verbs	Contractions	Other
kind	look for	I am = I'm	interesting
cashier	find	it is = it's	little
supermarket	keep	do not = don't	another
		that is = that's	
		you will = you'll	
		you are = you're	

Chris is a cashier at a supermarket. He doesn't like his job. It's not very interesting, and he doesn't make much money.

Gerry: What kind of work do you do?

Chris: I'm a cashier at a supermarket.

Gerry: Do you like your job?

Chris: No. It's not very interesting.

Gerry: And you don't make much money.

Chris: That's right. I make very little.

Gerry: I think you should look for another job.

Chris: I am, but it's not easy to find one.

Gerry: Keep looking! You'll get one.

Chris: Thanks. I hope you're right.

I. Comprehension

Answer these questions about the dialogue.

1. What kind of work does Chris do?
2. Does Chris like his job?
3. Why doesn't Chris like his job?
4. What is Chris looking for?
5. Is it difficult for Chris to find another job?
6. Does Gerry think Chris will find one?
*7. Chris tells his friend Gerry that he is looking for another job. Why is it a good idea to tell your friends when you're looking for a job?

II. Discussion: What About You?

Discuss these questions in pairs or small groups.

1. Is your job interesting?
2. How did you get your job?
3. If a person is looking for a job, what are some things the person should do?

III. Sentence Completion

Complete the sentences with these words.

kinds	looking for	cashier	interesting

1. That's a very _____ story.

2. Vince is _____ his wallet.

3. There are all _____ of animals in the zoo.

4. We pay the _____ when we leave.

another	find	little	keep

5. The _____ girl is running to her mother.

6. I'm going to have _____ cup of coffee.

7. _____ working! We have a lot more to do.

8. Did you _____ your ring?

IV. Paragraph Completion

Complete the paragraphs with these words.

little	cashier	interesting	kind

Chris is a _____ at a supermarket. He doesn't like this _____ of work because it isn't very _____ , and he makes very _____ money.

find	easy	another	keeps

Chris is looking for _____ job, but it's not _____ to _____ one. Gerry thinks that if Chris _____ looking, he'll get a job.

I Hate to Get Up

Listen to and pronounce these words.

Nouns	Verbs	Contractions	Other
morning	hate	do not = don't	me too
bookstore	get up	you are = you're	so
	have to		early
	has to		by
	be		until
	own		lucky

Pat gets up at six o'clock because she has to be to work by seven. Carol doesn't get up until eight.

Pat: I hate to get up in the morning!

Carol: Me too! What time do you get up?

Pat: At six o'clock.

Carol: Why do you get up so early?

Pat: I have to be at work by seven.

Carol: I don't get up until eight.

Pat: You're lucky! What do you do?

Carol: I own a bookstore.

Pat: What time does your store open?

Carol: At nine-thirty.

I. Comprehension

Answer these questions about the dialogue.

1. Does Pat like to get up in the morning?
2. What time does Pat get up?
3. Why does Pat get up so early?
4. What time does Carol get up?
5. What does Carol do?
6. What time does the store open?
*7. Pat is at work for eight hours. What time does Pat finish work?

II. Discussion: What About You?

Discuss these questions in pairs or small groups.

1. What time do you usually get up in the morning?
2. Is it difficult for you to get up in the morning?
3. Do you get up later on Saturday? On Sunday?

III. Sentence Completion

Complete the sentences with these words.

gets up   **so**   **early**   **hates**

1. Our bus is _____ today.

2. Sharon likes to eat, but she _____ to cook.

3. Your garden looks _____ pretty.

4. Mel _____ late when he's not working.

has to   **until**   **lucky**   **owns**

5. I'm going to wait _____ it stops raining.

6. Who _____ this bicycle?

7. Dave _____ go to the airport.

8. We have a beautiful day for the parade. We're _____ .

IV. Word Order

Make sentences of these words by putting them in the right order.

1. the morning / hate / in / I / to get up

   _____

2. get up / why / early / you / so / do / ?

   _____

3. be / seven / have to / by / I / at work

   _____

4. time / store / does / open / your / what / ?

   _____

A Busy Shoe Store

Listen to and pronounce these words.

Nouns		Verbs		Other	
nursery school	"Sesame Street"	learn	close	almost	before
letter	grade	count	stay	already	open
alphabet	shopping center	sell	order	eighth	or
swimming	shoe store	run	keep	next	sometimes
lesson	business	begin		together	both
				especially	

Paul and Rita are married and have two children, Eddie and Mary. Eddie is almost four years old. He goes to nursery school three days a week. He is learning the letters of the alphabet and can already count to ten. He also takes swimming lessons every Monday. "Sesame Street" is his favorite TV program. Mary is thirteen. She's in the eighth grade, and she'll go to high school next year. She's a very good student and wants to be a lawyer.

Paul and Rita own a shoe store; they sell children's shoes. They run the business together, and they work hard. Their store is in a shopping center. It's very busy, especially on Saturdays and the week before school begins. The store opens at ten in the morning and closes at six at night. On Thursdays it stays open until nine.

Paul or Rita is always in the store. Sometimes they're both there. Rita likes working with the children and their parents. Paul isn't very good at this. He takes care of ordering the shoes, paying the bills, and keeping the books.

I. Comprehension

Answer these questions about the story.

Paragraph 1

1. How often does Eddie go to nursery school?
2. What is he learning there?
3. What does he do every Monday?
4. What grade is Mary in? Where is she going next year?
5. What does she want to be?
*6. Eddie is learning the alphabet and his numbers at nursery school. What else do you think he is learning there?

Paragraph 2

1. What kind of store do Paul and Rita own?
2. Where is their store?
3. When is it especially busy?
4. What time does it open?
5. What time does it usually close? When does it close on Thursday?
*6. Why do you think it stays open late on Thursday?

Paragraph 3

1. Does Rita like working with the children and their parents?
2. Is Paul good at working with them?
3. What does Paul do at the store?

II. Discussion: What About You?

Discuss these questions in pairs or small groups.

1. Can you swim? Are you a good swimmer?
2. Did you ever take swimming lessons?
3. What is your favorite TV program?
4. Did you ever watch "Sesame Street"? What kind of program is it?
5. Do you often shop at shopping centers?
6. Name the shopping center or centers where you shop.
7. Name some of the stores that are in the shopping center where you shop.

III. Sentence Completion

Complete the sentences with these words.

almost	**lesson**	**learning**	**next**

1. Matthew has a piano _____ this afternoon.
2. When is the _____ plane to Atlanta?
3. It's _____ time to stop work.
4. The baby is _____ to walk.

begins	**or**	**counting**	**run**

5. Helen is _____ her money.
6. You can phone me at home _____ at work.
7. Mr. and Mrs. Gallo _____ the hotel.
8. The meeting _____ at ten o'clock.

together	**sell**	**stay**	**already**

9. Look! It's snowing _____ !
10. Does the store on the corner _____ newspapers?
11. The team plays very well _____ .
12. Souad's mother is coming from Syria. She's going to
    _____ with Souad for a month.

especially	**close**	**both**	**order**

13. _____ the door, please.
14. My wife likes cake, _____ chocolate cake.
15. I'm going to _____ a turkey sandwich. What are you getting?
16. The house has two bedrooms, and _____ are large.

Quiet and Very Serious

Listen to and pronounce these words.

Nouns	Verbs		Other	
joke	smile	hit	however	for long
	kid	shout	angry	strict
	make	forget	quickly	only
	laugh	correct	serious	true
	fight	obey	completely	necessary
			rarely	patient

Paul loves his wife and children very much, and they love him. However, it's not easy to live with Paul. He gets angry quickly, and he doesn't smile much. He's quiet and very serious. Paul doesn't have many friends.

Rita is completely different. She's always smiling and kidding. She likes to tell jokes and make people laugh. She's never quiet for long, and she rarely gets angry. She has many friends.

Paul and Rita are happy, but they often fight about the children. Rita thinks Paul is too strict with them. He never hits them, but he shouts at them a lot. He forgets that they're only children, and he's always correcting them. Eddie and Mary are afraid of their father. When they want something, they go to their mother.

Paul thinks Rita is too easy with the children. He says she lets them do anything they want, but that's not true. She corrects them when it's necessary, and they listen to her. She doesn't shout at her children, but they obey her. She's very kind and patient.

I. Comprehension

Answer these questions about the story.

Paragraph 1

1. Is Paul easy to live with?
2. Does he get angry quickly?
3. Does he have a lot of friends?

Paragraph 2

1. What does Rita like to do?
2. Does she have a lot of friends?
3. Why does Rita have many friends and Paul have only a few?

Paragraph 3

1. What do Paul and Rita fight about?
2. Is Paul strict with his children? Does he ever hit them?
3. Why are Eddie and Mary afraid of their father?
4. When they want something, where do they go?
*5. Do you think Paul is too strict with his children? Give a reason for your answer.

Paragraph 4

1. Does Rita let the children do anything they want?
2. When does she correct them?
3. Do the children listen to and obey her?
*4. Do you think mothers or fathers are usually stricter with their children? Give a reason for your answer.

II. Discussion: What About You?

Discuss these questions in pairs or small groups.

1. Do you get angry quickly?
2. Do you like to tell jokes?
3. Are you good at telling jokes?
4. Some people think that parents should never hit their children. Do you think there are times when it's okay for a parent to hit a child?
5. Are you easy or strict with children? Are you more like Rita or Paul?
6. Do you think it's good for children to be afraid of their parents? Give a reason for your answer.
7. Were you afraid of your mother? Your father?

III. Sentence Completion

Complete the sentences with these words.

| **fight** | **smile** | **quickly** | **forget** |

1. Don't _____ your eyeglasses!

2. Irene and Melissa are good friends, and they never

   _____ .

3. We don't have much time. We have to work _____ .

4. _____ , please! I want to take your picture.

| **kidding** | **shouts** | **completely** | **obey** |

5. Everything in the office is _____ new.

6. I tell people that I'm sixteen, but they know that I'm

   _____ .

7. Children should _____ their parents.

8. We don't like it when the boss _____ at us.

| **true** | **angry** | **hit** | **jokes** |

9. Did the ball _____ the window?

10. There are some good _____ in this magazine.

11. I'm _____ at Phil because he didn't help us.

12. Is it _____ that Doris is going to marry Jeff?

| **correct** | **afraid** | **laugh** | **however** |

13. Marty is always nice. No one is _____ of him.

14. Margaret has some money in the bank. _____ , she
    isn't rich.

15. When our son does something bad, we _____ him.

16. We like that TV program; it makes us _____ .

WORD REVIEW

Synonyms

Synonyms are words that have the same or similar meanings. Next to the sentences, write a synonym for the underlined word or words.

terrific   **wants**   **kind**   **keep**

1. What <u>type</u> of person is Stanley? _____

2. That was a <u>great</u> dinner! _____

3. <u>Continue</u> studying! You're learning a lot. _____

4. Karen <u>wishes</u> to move to California. _____

owns   **order**   **quickly**   **glad**

5. I'm going to <u>ask for</u> steak and french fries. _____

6. We're <u>happy</u> you can go with us. _____

7. Henry <u>has</u> two dogs and a cat. _____

8. Denise talks <u>fast</u>. _____

Antonyms

Antonyms are words that have opposite meanings. In the blank spaces, write an antonym for each word.

wrong   **hate**   **friend**   **get up**

1. love _____   3. go to bed _____

2. right _____   4. enemy _____

laugh   **true**   **forget**   **live**

5. die _____   7. remember _____

6. false _____   8. cry _____

6

The Weather

A Hot Day

Listen to and pronounce these words.

Nouns	Verbs	Contractions	Other
heat	kill	I will = I'll	ninety-five
degree	must		lazy
weather	would like		cooler
	taste		until
	hate		
	sleep		

It's a very hot day. Terry and Gene don't like hot weather. Gene gets Terry a cold drink, and they talk about the heat.

Terry: This heat is killing me!

Gene: Me too! It must be ninety-five degrees.

Terry: I would like a cold drink.

Gene: I'll get you one.

Terry: Thanks. Mmm. This tastes good!

Gene: I hate to work in hot weather.

Terry: I do too. It makes me lazy.

Gene: And it makes it hard to sleep.

Terry: When are we getting cooler weather?

Gene: Not until next week.

I. Comprehension

Answer these questions about the dialogue.

1. What is killing Terry?
2. How hot does Gene say it must be?
3. What does Terry want?
4. How does the drink taste?
5. How does the weather make Terry feel?
6. When will the weather be cooler?
*7. Why should people drink more when the weather is hot?

II. Discussion: What About You?

Discuss these questions in pairs or small groups.

1. Do you like hot weather?
2. Does hot weather make you feel lazy?
3. What do you like to drink when it's hot?

III. Sentence Completion

Complete the sentences with these words.

killing   **would**   **lazy**   **taste**

1. We're going swimming. _____ you like to come?

2. This toothache is _____ me!

3. How does the meat _____ ?

4. Nelson doesn't have a job, and he isn't looking for one. He's

   _____ .

hates   **cooler**   **weather**   **must**

5. If the _____ is good this afternoon, I'm going for a
   walk.

6. Tony's store is doing well. He _____ be happy.

7. Lisa _____ to study for exams.

8. It'll be _____ in the morning.

IV. Paragraph Completion

Complete the paragraphs with these words.

would   **tastes**   **must**   **killing**

   It's a very hot day. It _____ be ninety-five degrees. The

heat is _____ Terry. He says he _____ like

a cold drink. Gene gets him one. It _____ good.

lazy   **until**   **hates**   **cooler**

Terry _____ to work in hot weather. It makes him

_____ . He's hoping for some _____

weather, but it's going to be very hot _____ next week.

Not a Cloud in the Sky

Listen to and pronounce these words.

Nouns	**Verb**	**Contractions**	**Other**
cloud	change	there is = there's	what a
sky		what is = what's	beautiful
temperature		it is = it's	too
degree			favorite
October			mine
fall			perfect
season			
leaf (singular)			
leaves (plural)			

Jackie and Robin are talking about the weather. It's a beautiful October day. Fall is their favorite season.

Jackie: What a beautiful day!

Robin: Yes, there's not a cloud in the sky.

Jackie: What's the temperature?

Robin: It's seventy degrees.

Jackie: I love October.

Robin: Me too. It's not too hot and not too cold.

Jackie: Fall is my favorite season.

Robin: Mine too.

Jackie: The weather is almost perfect.

Robin: And the leaves are very pretty when they change colors.

I. Comprehension

Answer these questions about the dialogue.

1. Is it a sunny day?
2. What's the temperature?
3. What month do Jackie and Robin love?
4. Why does Robin love October?
5. What is Jackie and Robin's favorite season?
6. Why are the leaves so pretty in the fall?
7. Does the *too* in "me *too*" have the same meaning as the *too* in "*too* hot"? If not, explain the different meanings.

II. Discussion: What About You?

Discuss these questions in pairs or small groups.

1. What is your favorite season? Why?
2. Is there a big difference between the weather in your country and the weather in the United States?
3. Do you like the weather in the United States?

III. Sentence Completion

Complete the sentences with these words.

there's	**favorite**	**mine**	**degrees**

1. This is my _____ sweater.

2. The water is only sixty _____ . It's too cold to swim in.

3. That's not Harry's pen. It's _____ .

4. _____ a small lake in the park.

season	**leaves**	**changes**	**temperature**

5. Beverly _____ her clothes when she comes home from school.

6. It's going to be warm today. The _____ is going up to seventy-five.

7. Jason and Kristin are playing in the _____ .

8. Summer is the _____ I like best.

IV. Word Order

Make sentences of these words by putting them in the right order.

1. the sky / there's / in / a cloud / not

   _____

2. favorite / my / is / season / fall

   _____

3. almost / is / weather / perfect / the

   _____

4. pretty / the leaves / very / are / when / colors / change / they

   _____

Cold and Windy

Listen to and pronounce these words.

Nouns	Verbs	Contractions	Other
post office	wear	it is = it's	out
package	mail	I am = I'm	windy
stamp	would	I will = I'll	heavy
	buy	here is = here's	how many
			(be) back

Carol is going to the post office to mail a package. Lynn asks her to buy some stamps.

Carol: Is it cold out?

Lynn: Yes, it's cold and windy!

Carol: I'm going to wear my heavy coat.

Lynn: Good idea! Where are you going?

Carol: To the post office.

Lynn: Why?

Carol: To mail this package.

Lynn: Would you buy some stamps for me?

Carol: Sure. How many do you want?

Lynn: Ten. Here's the money for the stamps.

Carol: Okay. I'll be back in twenty minutes.

I. Comprehension

Answer these questions about the dialogue.

1. Is it cold out?
2. What is Carol going to wear?
3. Where is Carol going?
4. Why is Carol going to the post office?
5. What does Lynn ask Carol to buy?
6. How many stamps does Lynn want?
*7. Lynn is going to use the stamps to send letters within the United States. How much will the stamps cost?

II. Discussion: What About You?

Discuss these questions in pairs or small groups.

1. Do you go to the post office much?
2. Is it difficult for you to speak English when you go to the post office?
3. How much does it cost to send a letter to your country?

III. Sentence Completion

Complete the sentences with these words.

wear   **windy**   **mail**   **out**

1. Please _____ this letter for me.
2. The dog wants to go _____ .
3. I don't know what to _____ to the party.
4. It's raining and it's very _____ .

buy   **would**   **back**   **heavy**

5. This box is _____ . What's in it?
6. You can't _____ much with five dollars today.
7. When will Eileen be _____ ?
8. _____ you get me a glass of water, please?

IV. Paragraph Completion

Complete the paragraphs with these words.

wearing   **out**   **post office**   **windy**

Carol is going to the _____ . It's cold _____ and it's also _____ . Carol is _____ a warm coat.

heavy   **back**   **buy**   **mail**

Carol is going to _____ a _____ package. She's also going to _____ some stamps for Lynn. She'll be _____ in twenty minutes.

It's Beginning to Snow

Listen to and pronounce these words.

Nouns	**Verbs**	**Contractions**	**Other**
snow	hate	do not = don't	so
mile	begin	it is = it's	well
inch	snow		how
			far
			about
			dangerous

Stacy likes snow because it's pretty. Lee hates snow because he doesn't like to drive in it.

Stacy: Do you like snow?

Lee: No! I hate it!

Stacy: Why? Snow is so pretty.

Lee: Yes, but I don't like to drive in it.

Stacy: Well, it's beginning to snow.

Lee: And I have to drive to work.

Stacy: How far is it to work?

Lee: Five miles. Are we going to get much snow?

Stacy: About ten inches, they say.

Lee: Oh no! Driving will be dangerous!

I. Comprehension

Answer these questions about the dialogue.

1. Does Lee like snow?
2. Why does Stacy like snow?
3. Why doesn't Lee like snow?
4. What is it beginning to do?
5. What does Lee have to do?
6. How far is it to Lee's work?
*7. Stacy says they're going to get about ten inches of snow. How do you think Stacy knows this?

II. Discussion: What About You?

Discuss these questions in pairs or small groups.

1. Do you like snow?
2. Does it get very cold in your country in winter?
3. Do you get much snow in your country?

III. Sentence Completion

Complete the sentences with these words.

so	hates	how	begin

1. _____ bad was the accident?

2. The movie will _____ in ten minutes.

3. My son is five years old, and he _____ to go to bed.

4. Why are you driving _____ slow?

far	about	inches	dangerous

5. Bernie weighs _____ two hundred pounds.

6. Is it _____ to the hospital?

7. Playing with a gun is very _____ .

8. There are thirty-six _____ in a yard.

IV. Word Order

Make sentences of these words by putting them in the right order.

1. like / snow / I / to drive / don't / in

   _____

2. work / have to / I / to / drive

   _____

3. are / snow / get / we / much / going to / ?

   _____

4. be / driving / dangerous / will

   _____

From Santiago to New York

Listen to and pronounce these words.

Nouns		Verbs	Other
Santiago	aunt	stay	still
Dominican Republic	uncle	own	until
Manhattan	pay	seem	almost
New York City	English	cry	impossible
United States	American	dream	warm
Broadway	apartment	go back	friendly
part	friend	there are	
grocery store			

Sandra is twenty years old. She comes from Santiago, a city in the Dominican Republic. She lives with her aunt and uncle and three cousins in Manhattan, which is part of New York City. Her parents and two brothers still live in Santiago. Her brothers want to come to the United States, but her parents are going to stay in Santiago.

Sandra works in a small grocery store on Broadway. Her cousin owns the store. She works six days a week from ten in the morning until eight at night. The job isn't hard, but the hours are long and the pay is low. Sandra wants to get a better job, but she doesn't know any English. If you don't know English, it's almost impossible to get a good job.

Life in New York City isn't easy for Sandra. The weather is cold; the Americans seem cold; and sometimes her apartment is cold. When she comes home from work, she thinks about her parents, brothers, and friends in Santiago. Sometimes she cries a little. She dreams of going back, but she can't. In Santiago the weather is warm and the people are friendly, but there are no jobs there for Sandra.

I. Comprehension

Answer these questions about the story.

Paragraph 1

1. What country is Sandra from?
2. Who does she live with?
3. Where does she live?
*4. Why do you think her parents are going to stay in Santiago?

Paragraph 2

1. Where does Sandra work?
2. Who owns the store she works in?
3. How many days a week does she work?
4. How many hours a day does she work?
5. Why can't she get a better job?

Paragraph 3

1. What is the problem with the weather in New York?
2. How do the Americans seem to Sandra?
3. Who does she think about when she comes home?
4. What does she dream about?
5. Why can't she go back to Santiago?
*6. Why do you think Americans seem cold to Sandra? Do Americans seem cold to you?

II. Discussion: What About You?

Discuss these questions in pairs or small groups.

1. In what city did you live in your country?
2. What city do you live in now?
3. Compare these two cities. How are they different? Are they the same in some ways?
4. Is not knowing English well a big problem for you? Give a reason for your answer.
5. Did you ever go back to your country for a visit?
6. Do you ever dream of going back to live in your country?
7. Do you think you will ever go back to live there?

III. Sentence Completion

Complete the sentences with these words.

uncle	**still**	**grocery**	**stay**

1. Is Eva _____ talking on the telephone?

2. We're going to _____ in a motel.

3. Neil is my _____ . He's my father's brother.

4. There is a _____ store near my house.

if	**owns**	**until**	**seem**

5. My sister _____ a small restaurant.

6. _____ you need anything, call me.

7. Ruth and Fred _____ to be very happy.

8. I won't see Donna _____ tomorrow.

cry	**almost**	**dream**	**sometimes**

9. _____ my husband cooks supper.

10. Don't _____ ! Everything will be okay.

11. I _____ about Paula a lot. I love her.

12. It's March 15th. Spring is _____ here.

there are	**friendly**	**going back**	**have to**

13. Is Mildred _____ to school in September?

14. _____ some stamps in my desk.

15. I don't _____ work this Saturday.

16. Roy speaks to everyone; he's very _____ .

Sandra Can't Wait

Listen to and pronounce these words.

Nouns		Verbs		Other
money order	letter	save	get married	every
department store	time	send	answer	also
beach	taxi	shop	cost	yet
summer	visa	learn	arrive	immediately
		teach		soon

There are many things about living in the United States that Sandra likes. She can save money and can also send her parents a small money order every week. She likes to shop in the big department stores. She likes to go to the beach in the summer. She is learning to drive. Her cousin is teaching her, and she uses his car. She doesn't have a car yet.

Sandra has a boyfriend in Santiago, and she loves him very much. His name is Roberto and he's also twenty. Sandra and Roberto plan to get married, but they don't know when. Sandra writes a long letter to Roberto every week. He answers her letter immediately. She reads his letters three or four times and saves them.

Roberto drives a taxi in Santiago, but he doesn't make a lot of money. Taxis don't cost much in Santiago. Roberto plans to come to the United States soon. He's waiting for his visa. He has a brother and two sisters in New York. Sandra can't wait for the day Roberto arrives. She loves him so much.

I. Comprehension

Answer these questions about the story.

Paragraph 1

1. What does Sandra send her parents every week?
2. Where does she like to shop?
3. Where does she like to go in the summer?
4. What is she learning to do?
*5. Why do you think she doesn't have a car yet?

Paragraph 2

1. Are Roberto and Sandra the same age?
2. Do they know when they're going to get married?
3. How often does Sandra write to Roberto?
4. Does he answer her letters quickly?
5. What does Sandra do with his letters after she reads them? *Why?

Paragraph 3

1. What does Roberto do?
2. Are taxis expensive in Santiago?
3. Why doesn't Roberto come to the United States immediately?
4. Why can't Sandra wait for him to arrive?
*5. Do you think Sandra and Roberto will get married soon after he comes to New York? Give a reason for your answer.

II. Discussion: What About You?

Discuss these questions in pairs or small groups.

1. Are your parents living?
2. If they are, do they live in the United States or in your country?
3. What do you like about living in the United States?
4. What don't you like about living in the United States?
5. Do you write to anyone in your country? If you do, who do you write to?
6. Is anyone in your family planning to come to the United States?
7. Is it easy or difficult for people in your country to get a visa to come to the United States?

III. Sentence Completion

Complete the sentences with these words.

yet   **money order**   **beach**   **send**

1. Esther is going to be eighteen this week. We should

   _____ her a birthday card.

2. You can get a _____ at the bank or post office.

3. Do you want to go to the _____ with me? It's going to
   be a sunny day.

4. My daughter is four. She doesn't go to school _____ .

shop   **department store**   **also**   **get married**

5. Ben speaks French well. He's _____ studying Russian.

6. Today is a good day to _____ . There are a lot of sales.

7. I think Bob and Marlene are too young to _____ .

8. You can buy almost anything in a _____ .

times   **answer**   **cost**   **soon**

9. Please _____ the doorbell.

10. It's seven-thirty. Larry will be home _____ .

11. Greg phones his girlfriend five or six _____ a week.

12. How much does it _____ to fly to Rome?

visa   **arrives**   **save**   **every**

13. I'm going to _____ these coupons. I can use them.

14. Garry walks to work _____ day.

15. Our train _____ in Boston at 11:00 A.M.

16. Bhanu is going to India to visit her parents. She has to get a

   _____ .

WORD REVIEW

Synonyms

Synonyms are words that have the same or similar meanings. Next to the sentences, write a synonym for the underlined word or words.

begin	about	be back	immediately

1. Rached will <u>return</u> tomorrow. _____
2. What time do you <u>start</u> work? _____
3. Christina needs a doctor <u>now</u>. _____
4. I use <u>almost</u> ten gallons of gas a week. _____

fall	soon	friendly	arrive

5. Did Craig <u>come</u> yet? _____
6. Summer ends and <u>autumn</u> begins in September.

   _____

7. Your dog is <u>nice</u>. I like him. _____
8. Gladys will be here <u>in a short time</u>. _____

Antonyms

Antonyms are words that have opposite meanings. In the blank spaces, write an antonym for each word.

hard	dangerous	out	far

1. safe _____   3. easy _____
2. near _____   4. in _____

low	come from	a little	save

5. spend _____   7. high _____
6. go to _____   8. a lot _____

7

Sports and Fun

A House at the Shore

Listen to and pronounce these words.

Nouns	**Verbs**	**Contractions**	**Other**
vacation	start	we are = we're	next
shore	rent	that is = that's	wonderful
ocean	swim		then
beach	lie (on)		

Fran and his wife are starting their vacation next week. They're renting a house at the shore. They don't swim much, but they love to lie on the beach.

Chris: When is your vacation?

Fran: It starts next week.

Chris: Where are you going?

Fran: We're renting a house at the shore.

Chris: That's wonderful!

Fran: Yes, we love the ocean.

Chris: Do you swim a lot?

Fran: Not very much.

Chris: Then, why are you going to the shore?

Fran: We love to lie on the beach.

I. Comprehension

Answer these questions about the dialogue.

1. When does Fran's vacation start?
2. Is Fran going to stay home for his vacation?
3. Where is Fran renting a house?
4. Does Chris think it's a good idea to rent a house at the shore?
5. Does Fran swim a lot?
6. Why is Fran going to the shore?
*7. Lying on the beach can be dangerous. Why?

II. Discussion: What About You?

Discuss these questions in pairs or small groups.

1. What do you do on your vacation? Do you usually stay home or go somewhere?
2. Do you live near the ocean? Do you ever go to the shore? Do you go often?
3. Do you go swimming much? Where do you go swimming?

III. Sentence Completion

Complete the sentences with these words.

vacation   **shore**   **rent**   **next**

1. Who's _____ ? Who can I help?

2. We like the New Jersey _____ . It has many pretty beaches.

3. Have a nice _____ !

4. We'll _____ a car when we get to San Diego.

then   **lie on**   **start**   **wonderful**

5. How did the fire _____ ?

6. Mrs. Ditka is a _____ person. You'll like her.

7. Louise doesn't smoke. _____ , why is she buying cigarettes?

8. The dog likes to _____ Ernie's bed.

IV. Paragraph Completion

Complete the paragraphs with these words.

rent   **vacation**   **shore**   **starts**

Fran is thinking about his _____ . It _____ on Monday. He's going to _____ a house at the

_____ .

wonderful   **ocean**   **next**   **lie on**

Fran doesn't like to swim in the _____ , but he likes to _____ the beach. That's what he'll be doing _____ week. He's going to have a _____ time.

A Picnic

Listen to and pronounce these words.

Nouns	**Verbs**	**Contractions**	**Other**
picnic	let (us)	let us = let's	great
mile	shall	that is = that's	far
lake	bring	I will = I'll	about
sandwich			beautiful
cookie			
kid			

Pat and Gerry are going to a park for a picnic. Gerry is going to make some sandwiches, and Pat is going to bring soda and cookies.

Pat: Let's go for a picnic.

Gerry: That's a great idea! Where shall we go?

Pat: Let's go to the park.

Gerry: How far is it?

Pat: About a mile.

Gerry: Is it a nice place?

Pat: Sure. It has picnic tables and a beautiful lake.

Gerry: Good. I'll make some sandwiches.

Pat: I'll bring soda and cookies.

Gerry: The kids will love it.

I. Comprehension

Answer these questions about the dialogue.

1. What does Pat want to do?
2. Where does Pat want to go?
3. How far is the park?
4. Why is the park a nice place for a picnic?
5. What is Gerry going to make?
6. What is Pat going to bring?
*7. Why do you think children love picnics?

II. Discussion: What About You?

Discuss these questions in pairs or small groups.

1. Do you like picnics? Do you sometimes go on a picnic?
2. Where do you go for a picnic?
3. Who goes with you? What do you take to eat and drink?

III. Sentence Completion

Complete the sentences with these words.

great	**let's**	**far**	**shall**

1. What _____ we do tonight?
2. Pablo Picasso was a _____ artist.
3. It's not _____ to the barbershop. I can walk.
4. We're late. _____ take a taxi.

kids	**beautiful**	**bring**	**about**

5. Laura is a _____ girl.
6. There are _____ twenty students in our class.
7. The _____ are making a snowman.
8. Come to the party and _____ a friend.

IV. Word Order

Make sentences of these words by putting them in the right order.

1. park / go / the / let's / to

   _____

2. place / a / it / nice / is / ?

   _____

3. make / sandwiches / I'll / some

   _____

4. will / it / kids / love / the

   _____

I'm Going Skiing

Listen to and pronounce these words.

Nouns	Verbs	Contractions	Other
fun	have got	we have got = we've got	wow
	ski	that is = that's	terrific
	go skiing	what is = what's	serious
	worry	I am = I'm	maybe
		I will = I'll	dangerous
		it is = it's	too
		do not = don't	careful

They have ten inches of snow where Terry lives, and she is going skiing. Carol tells her that skiing is dangerous. Terry says she'll be careful.

Carol: We've got ten inches of snow.

Terry: Wow! That's terrific!

Carol: What's so terrific about it?

Terry: I'm going skiing.

Carol: Skiing? Are you serious?

Terry: Yes. It's a lot of fun.

Carol: Maybe, but it's also dangerous.

Terry: It's dangerous to drive a car, too.

Carol: Yes, but we have to drive. We don't have to ski.

Terry: Don't worry! I'll be careful.

I. Comprehension

Answer these questions about the dialogue.

1. How many inches of snow do they have?
2. Is Terry happy about the snow?
3. Is Carol happy about the snow?
4. What is Terry going to do?
5. What does Terry say about skiing?
6. What does Carol say about skiing?
7. Carol knows that both driving and skiing are dangerous, but she says there is a big difference between the two. What is the difference?

II. Discussion: What About You?

Discuss these questions in pairs or small groups.

1. Did you ever ski? Do you ski now? Where?
2. Are there places in your country to ski or is it too warm? Do many people go skiing in your country?
3. Why is it dangerous to ski?

III. Sentence Completion

Complete the sentences with these words.

maybe   **have got**   **terrific**   **fun**

1. We have _____ when we play basketball.
2. *The King and I* was a _____ play and movie.
3. Elaine has a car. _____ she can drive us home.
4. We _____ a computer in our office.

dangerous   **too**   **careful**   **worries**

5. Marie and Denis are getting a new refrigerator. We need a new one,

   _____ .

6. Swimming in the ocean can be _____ .
7. Barbara _____ a lot about her children.
8. There are eggs in that bag. Be _____ !

IV. Paragraph Completion

Complete the paragraphs with these words.

serious   **maybe**   **have got**   **fun**

They _____ ten inches of snow or _____
more where Terry and Carol live. Terry likes to ski. It's _____.
Terry tells Carol she's going skiing. Carol thinks she's kidding, but she
isn't. She's _____ .

too   **careful**   **worry**   **dangerous**

Carol doesn't want Terry to go skiing because it's _____ ,
but driving is _____ and we don't stop driving. Terry tells
Carol not to _____ . She'll be _____ .

A Soccer Game

Listen to and pronounce these words.

Nouns	**Verbs**	**Contractions**	**Other**
soccer	begin	I am = I'm	who
player	hope	do not = don't	best
team	win	can not = can't	busy
game			later

Sandy is going to play soccer with some friends from work. Sandy asks Lynn to come to the game, but she can't. She's very busy.

Sandy: I'm going to play soccer.

 Lynn: Who are you playing with?

Sandy: Some friends from work.

 Lynn: Are you a good soccer player?

Sandy: Yes, but I'm not the best player on the team.

 Lynn: What time does the game begin?

Sandy: Ten o'clock. Why don't you come with me?

 Lynn: I can't today. I'm very busy.

Sandy: Okay. See you later.

 Lynn: I hope your team wins.

I. Sentence Completion

Answer these questions about the dialogue.

1. What is Sandy going to do?
2. Who is Sandy going to play with?
3. Is Sandy a good soccer player?
4. What time does the game begin?
5. Is Lynn going to the game?
6. Why can't Lynn go to the game?
*7. Why do you think soccer is so popular in so many countries?

II. Discussion: What About You?

Discuss these questions in pairs or small groups.

1. Did you ever play soccer?
2. Do you play soccer now? Do you play for a team?
3. Is soccer a popular sport in your country? Is it the most popular sport?

III. Sentence Completion

Complete the sentences with these words.

soccer	**best**	**team**	**begin**

1. Our school has a very good baseball _____ .
2. When does the parade _____ ?
3. Doctor Hill is one of the _____ doctors in the city.
4. In most countries the game is called "futbol"; in the United States it's called _____ .

busy	**hope**	**later**	**win**

5. Brian and Roseann _____ to go to Puerto Rico this summer.
6. Sal isn't hungry. He's going to eat _____ .
7. We live on a _____ street.
8. If you play well, you will _____ .

IV. Word Order

Make sentences of these words by putting them in the right order.

1. soccer / I'm / play / going to

   _____

2. good / you / player / are / soccer / a / ?

   _____

3. begin / time / the game / what / does / ?

   _____

4. your / wins / hope / team / I

   _____

Peace and Quiet

Listen to and pronounce these words.

Nouns			**Verbs**	**Other**
clothes	country	pack	go fishing	away
feeling	swimmer	leave	go swimming	north
Miami	afternoon	build	sell	often
Florida	yard	repair	spend	alone
carpenter	real estate	enjoy	relax	excellent
peace	family	fish		during
quiet				

Harry and Nancy are packing their clothes; their vacation begins tomorrow. They're going to be away for three weeks. It's a wonderful feeling. They live in Miami, Florida, and they're renting a house on a small lake about one hundred miles north of the city. They're leaving tomorrow at nine in the morning.

Harry is a carpenter and a hard worker. He often works ten hours a day. He helps to build new houses and repair old ones. He likes his job and the city, but he also enjoys the peace and quiet of the country. He loves to fish. He rents a boat and goes fishing on the lake for four or five hours. He usually goes with a friend, but sometimes he goes alone.

Nancy doesn't like to fish, but she's an excellent swimmer. She goes swimming every afternoon. After she swims, she sits in the yard and reads for a few hours. Nancy sells real estate. She spends a lot of time in her office and taking people to see houses. Her job and her family keep her busy. She doesn't get much time to read and relax during the year.

I. Comprehension

Answer these questions about the story.

Paragraph 1

1. What are Harry and Nancy doing?
2. When does their vacation start?
3. How long are they going to be away?
4. Where do they live?
5. Where are they going for their vacation?

Paragraph 2

1. What is Harry's job?
2. What does he help to build?
3. Does he like the country?
4. What does he love to do?
*5. Do you think it's more fun to fish alone or with someone else? Why? Which does Harry like better?

Paragraph 3

1. Does Nancy like to fish?
2. What does she do every afternoon?
3. What does she do after she swims?
4. What does she sell?
*5. Do you think it's easy or difficult to sell real estate? Why?

II. Discussion: What About You?

Discuss these questions in pairs or small groups.

1. Did you ever live in the country? Do you live there now?
2. What are some good things about living in the country?
3. What are some good things about living in the city?
4. Do you ever go fishing? Do you fish much? Where?
5. Are you busy a lot?
6. What keeps you busy?
7. Do you or did you ever have a job selling things? If so, what do or did you sell?

III. Sentence Completion

Complete the sentences with these words.

leave   **feeling**   **pack**   **build**

1. The city is going to _____ a new high school.

2. Shall we _____ a lunch or eat at McDonald's?

3. What time does Jennifer _____ for work?

4. I have a _____ that Lorenzo doesn't like me.

repair   **enjoy**   **quiet**   **often**

5. It's a good book. You'll _____ it.

6. Do you see your brother _____ ?

7. Jeanette says she can _____ the chair.

8. The house is _____ when the children aren't home.

country   **peace**   **carpenter**   **excellent**

9. Dan is making new cabinets for our kitchen. He's a

_____ .

10. The air in the _____ is cleaner than in the city.

11. Edith is an _____ writer.

12. We want _____ , not war.

spend   **relax**   **real estate**   **sells**

13. On Sunday, I like to read the newspapers and _____ .

14. Victor wants to study; he's going to _____ the afternoon in the library.

15. We're looking for a store that _____ bicycles.

16. Agnes owns a lot of _____ . She's rich.

No Children This Year

Listen to and pronounce these words.

Nouns		Verbs	Other	
cards	woods	stay up	first	long
couple	air	be able	without	usually
town	noise	forget	away from	together
state park	shop		lonely	few
			both	fresh

This is the first year that Nancy and Harry are going on vacation without any of their children. Their son is away at college this summer, and their two daughters are married. They feel a little lonely without the children, but it's nice, too. They don't have to worry about where the children are or what they're doing.

Both Harry and Nancy are good cooks. Nancy cooks one night, and Harry cooks the next. After they do the dishes, they watch TV or they play cards with the couple next door. Sometimes they drive to town to see a movie. They usually stay up at night and sleep late in the morning.

Nancy and Harry also like to go for long walks together. There's a state park a few miles from their house. They drive to the park and walk in the woods. The air there is fresh, and the trees are pretty. It's good to be away from the heat and noise of Miami and to be able to forget the real estate office and the carpenter shop.

I. Comprehension

Answer these questions about the story.

Paragraph 1

1. Are Nancy and Harry's children with them?
2. Where is their son?
3. How do they feel without their children?
4. What don't they have to worry about on this vacation?
*5. Do you think most parents feel sad or happy, or both, when their children leave home? Give a reason for your answer.

Paragraph 2

1. Who does the cooking?
2. What do Nancy and Harry do after they finish the dishes?
3. Who do they play cards with?
4. Why do they drive to town sometimes?
5. Do they usually get up early in the morning?

Paragraph 3

1. How far is the state park from Nancy and Harry's house?
2. What do they do in the state park?
3. What are they happy to be away from?
4. What are they happy to forget?
*5. Why is it good for people to be away from their work for a few weeks?

II. Discussion: What About You?

Discuss these questions in pairs or small groups.

1. Do you think that everyone feels lonely sometimes?
2. Do you cook your own dinner or does someone cook for you?
3. Who does the dishes in your home?
4. Do you ever play cards? A lot?
5. Do you go to the movies much?
6. What was the last movie you saw? Was it good?
7. Do you like to stay up late? Do you stay up late often?

III. Sentence Completion

Complete the sentences with these words.

lonely	without	couple	together

1. Peggy and Blanche often play golf _____ .
2. Jean's wife is in Haiti. He feels _____ .
3. That young _____ dances very well.
4. I can't get to work _____ a car.

few	away from	both	usually

5. The cat is running _____ the dog.
6. Bill _____ goes to bed at eleven-thirty.
7. I know Joan and Connie well. _____ of them are my friends.
8. A _____ people are waiting for the store to open.

fresh	noise	stay up	woods

9. There are many birds and small animals in the _____ .
10. Linda is going to _____ and read tonight.
11. In the summer, the supermarket has a lot of _____ vegetables.
12. I hear a _____ in the kitchen.

long	be able	heat	forget

13. This room is cold. We need some _____ .
14. It was a _____ trip; I'm tired.
15. Don't _____ to phone us!
16. Will you _____ to take me to the airport?

WORD REVIEW

Synonyms

Synonyms *are words that have the same or similar meanings. Next to the sentences, write a synonym for the underlined word or words.*

busy   **fun**   **repair**   **relax**

1. Did you have <u>a good time</u> at the picnic? _____

2. We're going to the beach and <u>take it easy</u>. _____

3. Clara is <u>doing a lot</u> this morning. _____

4. Doug is going to <u>fix</u> the lamp. _____

enjoys   **often**   **wonderful**   **spend**

5. Hisako <u>frequently</u> comes to our house. _____

6. It's important to <u>use</u> your money well. _____

7. Ron <u>likes</u> class. _____

8. Our new VCR (video cassette recorder) is <u>very good</u>.

_____

Antonyms

Antonyms *are words that have opposite meanings. In the blank spaces, write an antonym for each word.*

best   **beautiful**   **win**   **north**

1. lose _____   3. south _____

2. ugly _____   4. worst _____

leave   **now**   **heat**   **noise**

5. later _____   7. cold _____

6. quiet _____   8. return _____

8

Schools and Children

Is English Difficult?

Listen to and pronounce these words.

Nouns	**Verbs**	**Contractions**	**Other**
country	learn	I am = I'm	difficult
Poland	have to	she is = she's	a lot
block	practice	it is = it's	kind
class			
fun			

Fran is from Poland. He's going to school to learn English. He likes his teacher. She's kind and class is fun.

Stacy: Where are you going?
Fran: To school to learn English.
Stacy: What country are you from?
Fran: I'm from Poland.
Stacy: Is English difficult?
Fran: Yes. I have to study and practice a lot.
Stacy: Where is your school?
Fran: It's three blocks from here.
Stacy: Do you like your teacher?
Fran: Yes, she's kind; class is fun.

I. Comprehension

Answer these questions about the dialogue.

1. Where is Fran going?
2. What country is Fran from?
3. Is English difficult for Fran?
4. What does Fran have to do?
5. How far is it to Fran's school?
6. Why does Fran like the teacher?
*7. Do you think students learn more when class is fun? Why?

II. Discussion: What About You?

Discuss these questions in pairs or small groups.

1. Do you study English much? How do you study it?
2. Do you practice English much? Who do you practice with?
3. Do you have fun in class?

III. Sentence Completion

Complete the sentences with these words.

           blocks   **learning**   **difficult**   **a lot**

1. Syd doesn't say much, but he thinks _____ .
2. How many _____ is it to the bank?
3. Math is a _____ subject for me.
4. Sheila is _____ to type.

           kind   **fun**   **practicing**   **have to**

5. It's _____ to swim.
6. I _____ brush my teeth.
7. The nurses in the hospital are very _____ .
8. Kim is _____ the piano.

IV. Paragraph Completion

Complete the paragraphs with these words.

           difficult   **learn**   **has to**   **blocks**

Fran is from Poland. He's going to school to _____ English. The school is three _____ from his house. English is a _____ language, and Fran _____ study hard.

           a lot of   **fun**   **kind**   **practices**

Fran has a good teacher. She's _____ to the students, and her class is _____ . When Fran goes home, he _____ English with his son. His first language is Polish, but he also knows _____ English.

A Lazy Boy

Listen to and pronounce these words.

Nouns	Verbs	Contractions	Other
surprise	say	I am = I'm	angry
teacher		he is = he's	well
		they are = they're	smart
		what is = what's	lazy
		that is = that's	maybe
			afraid
			so

Terry is angry at her son. He isn't doing well in school. He's smart, but he never studies. He's lazy.

Terry: I'm very angry at my son Jim.
Jackie: Why? What's the problem?
Terry: He's not doing well in school.
Jackie: That's a surprise. Jim is a smart boy.
Terry: Yes, but he never studies.
Jackie: Did you talk to his teachers?
Terry: Yes, I did.
Jackie: What did they say?
Terry: He's a nice boy, but he's very lazy.
Jackie: Maybe they're right.
Terry: I'm afraid so.

I. Comprehension

Answer these questions about the dialogue.

1. Who is Terry angry at?
2. Why is Terry angry?
3. Why is Jackie surprised that Jim isn't doing well in school?
4. Why isn't he doing well in school?
5. Did Terry talk to her son's teachers?
6. What did the teachers say?
*7. What do you think Terry should say to her son to get him to study?

II. Discussion: What About You?

Discuss these questions in pairs or small groups.

1. Do you get angry often? Sometimes? Almost never?
2. Can you think of something that your children, or your husband or wife, or other people do that makes you angry?
3. Are you lazy?

III. Sentence Completion

Complete the sentences with these words.

> **angry**   **surprise**   **smart**   **well**

1. We want Roger's birthday party to be a _____ .
2. Ann gets _____ when her daughter doesn't listen.
3. I like that band. They play _____ .
4. Shirley is a very good lawyer. She's _____ .

> **lazy**   **maybe**   **afraid**   **so**

5. _____ I'll get a haircut today.
6. Some people are _____ to drive at night.
7. They say the company is going to pay us more. If that's

   _____ , everyone will be happy.
8. Betty isn't _____ . She likes to work.

IV. Word Order

Make sentences of these words by putting them in the right order.

1. very / at / I'm / son / angry / my

   _____

2. well / school / he's / in / doing / not

   _____

3. boy / Jim / smart / a / is

   _____

4. talk / teachers / to / you / his / did / ?

   _____

Not So Young

Listen to and pronounce these words.

Nouns	**Verbs**	**Contractions**	**Other**
high school	graduate	she is = she's	next
	remember	we are = we're	how
	get married	do not = don't	true
		it is = it's	young
		is not = isn't	so
		that is = that's	

Carol's son is graduating from high school. Sandy's daughter is sixteen. Sandy says that he and Carol are getting old, but she doesn't think so.

Carol: My son is graduating from high school today!
Sandy: And my daughter is graduating next year.
Carol: How old is she?
Sandy: She's sixteen.
Carol: I remember when she was a baby.
Sandy: I know. We're getting old.
Carol: Don't say that!
Sandy: Why not? It's true.
Carol: No, it isn't! We were young when we got married.
Sandy: That's right, but we're not so young now.

I. Comprehension

Answer these questions about the dialogue.

1. When is Carol's son graduating from high school?
2. When is Sandy's daughter graduating?
3. How old is Sandy's daughter?
4. Does Sandy think that he and Carol are getting old?
5. Does Carol think that they're getting old?
6. Were Carol and Sandy young when they married?
*7. About how old do you think Carol and Sandy are?

II. Discussion: What About You?

Discuss these questions in pairs or small groups.

1. When do you think that a person is no longer young? At forty, fifty, sixty?
2. How old were you when you got married? How old should a couple be before they get married?
3. Do you think couples in your country usually marry at a younger age than couples in the United States?

III. Sentence Completion

Complete the sentences with these words.

> **young**   **graduate**   **true**   **how**

1. _____ hot is the water?

2. Keith is only twenty-five. He's a _____ man.

3. Is it _____ that you're moving to Hawaii?

4. When is Sally going to _____ from college?

> **remember**   **next**   **so**   **get married**

5. Ted loves Kathy and she loves him. I'm sure they'll

   _____ .

6. Our _____ class is Monday morning.

7. Dorothy doesn't feel _____ well.

8. I know that man, but I can't _____ his name.

IV. Paragraph Completion

Complete the paragraphs with these words.

> **graduating**   **got married**   **so**   **young**

Carol was _____ when she _____ , but
that was twenty years ago. Today her son is _____ from
high school. She's _____ happy.

> **true**   **next**   **how**   **remembers**

Carol asks Sandy _____ old his daughter is. She'll be
sixteen _____ week. Carol _____ when she
was a baby. Sandy says he and Carol are getting old, but she says that's
not _____ .

What's a Grant?

Listen to and pronounce these words.

Nouns	**Verbs**	**Contractions**	**Other**
college	must	that is = that's	great
grant	pay back	what is = what's	expensive
loan			between
government			
education			
difference			
gift			

Lee's daughter is going to college. It's expensive, but she has a grant. The grant doesn't pay for everything. She has a loan, too.

Lee: My daughter is going to college.

Chris: That's great, but it must be expensive.

Lee: Yes, but she has a grant.

Chris: A grant? What's a grant?

Lee: The government is giving her money.

Chris: To pay for her education?

Lee: That's right.

Chris: Does it pay for everything?

Lee: No, she has a loan, too.

Chris: What's the difference between a loan and a grant?

Lee: You have to pay back a loan; a grant is a gift.

I. Comprehension

Answer these questions about the dialogue.

1. Where is Lee's daughter going?
2. Does it cost a lot to go to college?
3. Who is giving the grant to Lee's daughter?
4. Does the grant pay for everything?
5. What else does Lee's daughter have?
6. What is the difference between a loan and a grant?
*7. Why do you think it's so expensive to go to college, especially a private college?

II. Discussion: What About You?

Discuss these questions in pairs or small groups.

1. What do you know about grants? Who does the government give grants to?
2. Where can you get information about grants?
3. Do you know anyone who received a grant to pay for his or her education?

III. Sentence Completion

Complete the sentences with these words.

expensive	great	must	grant

1. Alan didn't eat supper. He _____ be hungry.
2. I like the watch, but it's very _____ .
3. Nicole is getting a _____ to go to business school.
4. Abraham Lincoln was a _____ president.

government	loan	difference	pay back

5. We want to paint our house, but we don't have the money.
   We're going to ask for a _____ .
6. My brother lives in Washington; he works for the

   _____ .

7. Michelle and Cindy are sisters, but there's a big

   _____ in the way they act.
8. I have two years to _____ the money.

IV. Word Order

Make sentences of these words by putting them in the right order.

1. daughter / going / my / college / is / to

   _____

2. be / that's / must / it / expensive / but / great

   _____

3. money / giving / the government / her / is

   _____

4. pay back / you / loan / have to / a

   _____

Long Hours and
Hard Work

Listen to and pronounce these words.

Nouns		Verbs		Other
Philadelphia	Korean	own	hear	hard
fruit	housework	sell	speak	outside
vegetable	change	close	pronounce	too
Korea	sound	take care (of)	listen (to)	most
		understand		almost

Young Woo and Sun Ok are married, and they have two children, Tae Ho and Soo Jin. They live in Philadelphia, and they own a store that sells fruit and vegetables. They work very hard. The store opens at eight in the morning and closes at nine at night. It's doing well.

In Korea, Sun Ok never worked outside her home. Here she works in the store and has to take care of her family, too. Her husband helps with the housework, but she does most of the work at home, and he does most of the work in the store. Sun Ok likes to work in the store. It's a nice change from housework.

English is a big problem for Young Woo and Sun Ok. They understand everything they hear, but they can't speak well. It's almost impossible for them to pronounce the *l* and *r* sounds. They want to go to school to learn more English, but they don't have time now. Working in the store and listening to TV help them to learn English, but they speak Korean at home.

I. Comprehension

Answer these questions about the story.

Paragraph 1

1. Where do Young Woo and Sun Ok live?
2. What does their store sell?
3. What time does it open?
4. What time does it close?
5. How is it doing?

Paragraph 2

1. In what two places does Sun Ok work?
2. Who does most of the work at home?
3. Who does most of the work in the store?
4. Why does Sun Ok like to work in the store?
*5. Do you think Young Woo likes housework? Give a reason for your answer.

Paragraph 3

1. Is it easier for Young Woo and Sun Ok to understand English or to speak it?
2. What two sounds are difficult for them to pronounce?
3. Why don't they go to school?
4. What helps them to learn English?
*5. Why do you think they speak Korean and not English at home?

II. Discussion: What About You?

Discuss these questions in pairs or small groups.

1. If you are working, how many hours a day do you work?
2. Do married women in your country usually work outside their homes?
3. Do men in your country do much housework?
4. Who does the housework where you live?
5. Which is more difficult for you—to understand English or to speak it?
6. Are there any English letters that are especially difficult for you to pronounce? Which ones?
7. Do you speak your first language at home or do you speak English?

III. Sentence Completion

Complete the sentences with these words.

owns	**hard**	**close**	**outside**

1. _____ your books. We have a test today.

2. Rajiv _____ the red truck.

3. It's a nice day. Go _____ and play!

4. I'm going to take a taxi. It's raining very _____ .

too	**understand**	**never**	**take care of**

5. Sometimes we don't _____ what our teacher is saying.

6. My mother is sick. I'm going to stay home and _____ her.

7. George is a dentist, and his daughter wants to be a dentist, _____ .

8. Archie _____ wears a hat.

hear	**sells**	**changes**	**almost**

9. Brenda's store _____ clothing.

10. Hal is a good driver, but he _____ had an accident this morning.

11. Your plan is good, but we have to make some _____ in it.

12. Lucy is eighty-five years old. She doesn't _____ well.

pronounce	**housework**	**sound**	**listening to**

13. I like the _____ of your stereo.

14. Pamela is _____ a Bruce Springsteen tape.

15. My wife and I work during the day. We do the _____ at night.

16. How do you _____ this word?

Excellent Students

Listen to and pronounce these words.

Nouns		Verbs	Other
place	language	worry (about)	different
business	lesson	write down	half
fact	engineer	seem	excellent
respect	math =	pay attention	second
idea	mathematics		best
feeling	piano		
way			

Philadelphia is a good place for a business, but Young Woo and Sun Ok worry about their children. Schools are different in the United States. In Korea children listen and learn facts. They write down what the teacher says and study it. They have a lot of respect for their teachers. In the United States children seem to do what they want in school. They don't listen and do what the teacher says. Some children don't learn much.

Young Woo and Sun Ok's ideas and feelings are Korean. Their children's ideas and feelings are half Korean and half American. At home they learn Korean ways and the Korean language. In school and with their friends, they learn American ways and English. The children like school. They pay attention in class and study their lessons at home. They're excellent students.

Tae Ho is twelve and wants to be an engineer. He loves math and does very well in it. On Saturdays he helps his mother and father in the store. He also likes to play baseball. Soo Jin is seven, and she's in the second grade. She reads well and is one of the best students in the class. She likes music and takes piano lessons every week.

I. Comprehension

Answer these questions about the story.

Paragraph 1

1. Who do Young Woo and Sun Ok worry about?
2. What do students in Korean schools write down?
3. Do students in Korea have great respect for their teachers?
4. In the United States, what do children seem to do in school?
*5. Why do you think students in Korea show more respect for their teachers than students in the United States?

Paragraph 2

1. Are Young Woo and Sun Ok's ideas and feelings American or Korean?
2. Are their children's ideas and feelings American or Korean?
3. What do Tae Ho and Soo Jin learn at home?
4. What do they learn in school and with their friends?
*5. Why do you think that Tae Ho and Soo Jin are excellent students?

Paragraph 3

1. What does Tae Ho want to be?
2. What does he do on Saturday?
3. What sport does he like to play?
4. What grade is Soo Jin in?
5. What does she do every week?

II. Discussion: What About You?

Discuss these questions in pairs or small groups.

1. Everyone worries about something. What do you worry about sometimes?
2. Are schools in your country different from those in the United States? If so, how are they different?
3. Do you think children in your country have more respect for teachers than children in the United States? If so, why?
4. Do you think that schools in the United States are too easy?
5. Do you think that it's good for older children to work after school?
6. Did you ever take music lessons?
7. Can you play the piano or any musical instrument?

III. Sentence Completion

Complete the sentences with these words.

facts   **different**   **worries**   **business**

1. Tina _____ when her husband is late.
2. I like these shoes, but I want a _____ color.
3. Joan is going to start her own _____ .
4. Tell us what happened. We have to know the _____ .

respect   **half**   **ideas**   **seems**

5. The new mayor has some terrific _____ .
6. Pete _____ to like his job.
7. The plane will arrive in a _____ hour.
8. Everyone has _____ for Al. He's a very good person.

second   **pay attention**   **lessons**   **excellent**

9. The food at the restaurant was _____ .
10. _____ to what the doctor says!
11. The _____ part of the movie is better than the first.
12. Anita is taking dancing _____ .

ways   **engineers**   **feelings**   **best**

13. I hope I didn't hurt your _____ .
14. There are many _____ to learn a language.
15. It's the biggest and _____ park in the city.
16. The job of _____ is to plan buildings, roads, and bridges.

WORD REVIEW

Synonyms

Synonyms *are words that have the same or similar meanings. Next to the sentences, write a synonym for the underlined word or words.*

problem	**angry**	**maybe**	**be expensive**

1. The trip will cost a lot. _____
2. Why is Howie mad? _____
3. The difficulty with the book is that it's too long. _____
4. Are you going shopping tomorrow? Possibly. I don't know.

   _____

grant	**pronounce**	**sound**	**half**

5. What's making that noise? _____
6. The money is a gift. We don't have to pay it back.

   _____

7. Fifty percent of the students are from Latin America.

   _____

8. Did I say your name right? _____

Antonyms

Antonyms *are words that have opposite meanings. In the blank spaces, write an antonym for each word.*

well	**smart**	**graduate**	**more**

1. dumb _____   3. poorly _____
2. less _____   4. begin school _____

change	**excellent**	**child**	**take**

5. adult _____   7. give _____
6. very bad _____   8. be the same _____

Answer Key

1. Food

Page 4: A Good Cook

III. Sentence Completion

1. watching
2. where's
3. cooking
4. dinner
5. kitchen
6. can
7. tired
8. wife

IV. Paragraph Completion

1. kitchen
2. dinner
3. cooking
4. good
5. wife
6. can
7. tired
8. watching

Page 7: We Eat a Lot

III. Sentence Completion

1. again
2. if
3. key
4. on top of
5. a lot
6. package
7. busy
8. heavy

IV. Word Groups

1. yes   sure   okay
2. eat   drink   cook
3. with   to   on top of
4. bread   supermarket   apples
5. do   will   did

Page 10: A Little Milk but No Sugar

III. Sentence Completion

1. something
2. at night
3. please
4. never
5. awake
6. little
7. keep
8. relax

IV. Paragraph Completion

1. something
2. please
3. little
4. sugar
5. never
6. at night
7. awake
8. relax

Page 13: A Big Menu

III. Sentence Completion

1. getting
2. menu
3. vegetables
4. perfect
5. baked
6. fish
7. how about
8. any

IV. Word Groups

1. roast beef   hamburger   steak
2. butter   milk   cream
3. peas   lettuce   tomato
4. tea   soda   juice
5. menu   restaurant   food

Page 17: The Pizza Tastes Great

III. Sentence Completion

1. late
2. always
3. fast
4. favorite
5. early
6. weigh
7. diet
8. slowly
9. only
10. pounds
11. careful
12. so
13. different
14. thin
15. living room
16. calories

Page 20: Alice Loves to Shop and Talk

III. Sentence Completion

1. few	5. buying	9. listening	13. very
2. clothes	6. about	10. friendly	14. alone
3. because	7. news	11. shop	15. save
4. spend	8. also	12. same	16. fighting

Page 21: Word Review

Synonyms

1. little	5. few
2. can	6. dinner
3. great	7. watching
4. a lot	8. also

Antonyms

1. night	5. new
2. on top of	6. hot
3. never	7. fast
4. heavy	8. different

2. Health

Page 25: A Toothache

III. Sentence Completion

1. there	5. very
2. time	6. hear
3. o'clock	7. toothache
4. sure	8. sorry

IV. Paragraph Completion

1. time	5. toothache
2. o'clock	6. very
3. late	7. hears
4. there	8. sorry

Page 28: Sneezing a Lot

III. Sentence Completion

1. sleepy	5. better
2. soon	6. every
3. God	7. cold
4. feels	8. hope

IV. Word Groups

1. winter	spring	summer
2. doctor	dentist	nurse
3. feel	sleepy	tired
4. sneeze	cold	Contac
5. bless	love	help

Page 31: I Don't Feel Well

III. Sentence Completion

1. well	5. serious
2. looking for	6. later
3. appointment	7. fever
4. pain	8. nothing

IV. Paragraph Completion

1. looking for	5. appointment
2. well	6. serious
3. fever	7. nothing
4. pain	8. later

Page 34: A Sore Throat

III. Sentence Completion

1. sounds	5. so
2. terrible	6. stay
3. sore	7. hurts
4. voice	8. should

IV. Word Groups

1. today	tomorrow	yesterday
2. honey	sugar	candy
3. terrible	bad	no good
4. hurt	sore	pain
5. throat	neck	tongue

Page 38: A Doctor

III. Sentence Completion

1. have to
2. salesman
3. finish
4. smart
5. single
6. bill
7. go out
8. a lot
9. sell
10. another
11. department stores
12. graduate
13. marry
14. expensive
15. last
16. travel

Page 41: She Wants to Be Herself

III. Sentence Completion

1. herself
2. compare
3. like
4. angry
5. member
6. belongs
7. collect
8. ride
9. collection
10. still
11. hobby
12. know about
13. first
14. was
15. than
16. born

Page 42: Word Review

Synonyms

1. test
2. terrible
3. have to
4. stay
5. finish
6. smart
7. hard
8. rest

Antonyms

1. winter
2. well
3. late
4. bad
5. last
6. after
7. better
8. happy

3. Birthdays

Page 46: Good News

III. Sentence Completion

1. phones
2. great
3. so
4. news
5. me too
6. beginning
7. due
8. or

IV. Paragraph Completion

1. news
2. great
3. so
4. too
5. due
6. beginning
7. phone
8. say

Page 49: Is She Pretty?

III. Sentence Completion

1. too
2. birthday
3. age
4. cousins
5. pretty
6. how
7. too bad
8. married

IV. Word Groups

1. cousin   uncle   brother
2. pretty   handsome   beautiful
3. breakfast   lunch   dinner
4. party   gift   birthday
5. my   your   her

Page 52: A Cake

III. Sentence Completion

1. anything
2. near
3. is there
4. bakery
5. whose
6. else
7. get
8. pay

IV. Paragraph Completion

1. daughter
2. bakery
3. there is
4. near
5. time
6. else
7. pay
8. gets back

Page 55: A Birthday Present

III. Sentence Completion

1. of course	5. one
2. briefcase	6. let
3. yet	7. how about
4. got	8. different

IV. Word Groups

1. of course   clearly   sure
2. know   understand   think
3. shirt   tie   jacket
4. month   week   year
5. briefcase   notebook   pen

Page 58: Forty and Getting Gray

III. Sentence Completion

1. well	5. on fire
2. every	6. brave
3. getting	7. last
4. relax	8. still

9. jog	13. interesting
10. feel	14. insurance
11. computers	15. save
12. strong	16. pay attention

Page 62: On the Phone Too Much

III. Sentence Completion

1. change	5. hope
2. usually	6. best
3. all right	7. probably
4. subject	8. answer

9. passed	13. second
10. hard	14. magazine
11. inches	15. ringing
12. favorite	16. interests

Page 63: Word Review

Synonyms

1. phone	5. so
2. pretty	6. job
3. big	7. of course
4. all right	8. children

Antonyms

1. buy	5. stop
2. young	6. long
3. married	7. large
4. beginning	8. play

4. Cars and Planes

Page 67: Washing the Car

III. Sentence Completion

1. always	5. dirty
2. mess	6. again
3. in order	7. never
4. in front of	8. take care of

IV. Paragraph Completion

1. in front of	5. cleans
2. washing	6. always
3. takes	7. in order
4. care	8. mess

Page 70: Don't Worry

III. Sentence Completion

1. thanks	5. wait
2. kind	6. there is
3. officer	7. worry
4. try	8. hanger

IV. Word Groups

1. officer   policeman   cop
2. friendly   good   kind
3. truck   car   taxi
4. what   where   how
5. hanger   sweater   coat

Page 73: A Car Loan

III. Sentence Completion

1. wrong
2. loan
3. apply
4. a lot of
5. cash
6. about
7. have to
8. cost

IV. Paragraph Completion

1. driving
2. apply
3. loan
4. buy
5. wrong
6. has to
7. about
8. a lot of

Page 76: Afraid of Flying

III. Sentence Completion

1. afraid
2. understand
3. safe
4. meeting
5. maybe
6. flying
7. comfortable
8. foolish

IV. Word Groups

1. airport   fly   plane
2. foolish   stupid   crazy
3. men   people   women
4. Dallas   Saint Louis   Boston
5. meeting   appointment   time

Page 80: Two Boyfriends

III. Sentence Completion

1. mistakes
2. busy
3. file
4. lawyer
5. either
6. excellent
7. hurt
8. however
9. mechanic
10. fun
11. answer
13. soon
13. fix
14. fair
15. also
16. truth

Page 83: Will Linda Say Yes?

III. Sentence Completion

1. heavy
2. passengers
3. salary
4. wind
5. future
6. traffic
7. polite
8. eat out
9. hopes
10. appetite
11. difficult
12. wild
13. handsome
14. of course
15. usually
16. nervous

Page 84: Word Review

Synonyms

1. many
2. right
3. excellent
4. foolish
5. kind
6. however
7. mistake
8. handsome

Antonyms

1. open
2. nothing
3. easy
4. dirty
5. rich
6. truth
7. many
8. future

5. Work and Shopping

Page 88: On Sale

III. Sentence Completion

1. price
2. glad
3. on sale
4. looks
5. shopping
6. how much
7. terrific
8. too

IV. Paragraph Completion

1. looks
2. terrific
3. glad
4. how much
5. price
6. on sale
7. shop
8. too

Page 91: A New Dress

III. Sentence Completion

1. let
2. dear
3. wrong
4. full of
5. get
6. in style
7. closets
8. one

IV. Word Order

1. Don't you have your key?
2. You have a closet full of dresses.
3. What's wrong with all the other dresses?
4. They're not in style.

Page 94: A Cashier

III. Sentence Completion

1. interesting
2. looking for
3. kinds
4. cashier
5. little
6. another
7. keep
8. find

IV. Paragraph Completion

1. cashier
2. kind
3. interesting
4. little
5. another
6. easy
7. find
8. keeps

Page 97: I Hate to Get Up

III. Sentence Completion

1. early
2. hates
3. so
4. gets up
5. until
6. owns
7. has to
8. lucky

IV. Word Order

1. I hate to get up in the morning.
2. Why do you get up so early?
3. I have to be at work by seven.
4. What time does your store open?

Page 101: A Busy Shoe Store

III. Sentence Completion

1. lesson
2. next
3. almost
4. learning
5. counting
6. or
7. run
8. begins
9. already
10. sell
11. together
12. stay
13. close
14. especially
15. order
16. both

Page 104: Quiet and Very Serious

III. Sentence Completion

1. forget
2. fight
3. quickly
4. smile
5. completely
6. kidding
7. obey
8. shouts
9. hit
10. jokes
11. angry
13. true
13. afraid
14. however
15. correct
16. laugh

Page 105: Word Review

Synonyms

1. kind
2. terrific
3. keep
4. wants
5. order
6. glad
7. owns
8. quickly

Antonyms

1. hate
2. wrong
3. get up
4. friend
5. live
6. true
7. forget
8. laugh

6. The Weather

Page 109: A Hot Day

III. Sentence Completion

1. would
2. killing
3. taste
4. lazy
5. weather
6. must
7. hates
8. cooler

IV. Paragraph Completion

1. must
2. killing
3. would
4. tastes
5. hates
6. lazy
7. cooler
8. until

Page 112: Not a Cloud in the Sky

III. Sentence Completion

1. favorite
2. degrees
3. mine
4. there's
5. changes
6. temperature
7. leaves
8. season

IV. Word Order

1. There's not a cloud in the sky.
2. Fall is my favorite season.
3. The weather is almost perfect.
4. The leaves are very pretty when they change colors.

Page 115: Cold and Windy

III. Sentence Completion

1. mail
2. out
3. wear
4. windy
5. heavy
6. buy
7. back
8. would

IV. Paragraph Completion

1. post office
2. out
3. windy
4. wearing
5. mail
6. heavy
7. buy
8. back

Page 118: It's Beginning to Snow

III. Sentence Completion

1. how
2. begin
3. hates
4. so
5. about
6. far
7. dangerous
8. inches

IV. Word Order

1. I don't like to drive in snow.
2. I have to drive to work.
3. Are we going to get much snow?
4. Driving will be dangerous.

Page 122: From Santiago to New York

III. Sentence Completion

1. still
2. stay
3. uncle
4. grocery
5. owns
6. if
7. seem
8. until
9. sometimes
10. cry
11. dream
12. almost
13. going back
14. there are
15. have to
16. friendly

Page 125: Sandra Can't Wait

III. Sentence Completion

1. send
2. money order
3. beach
4. yet
5. also
6. shop
7. get married
8. department store
9. answer
10. soon
11. times
13. cost
13. save
14. every
15. arrives
16. visa

Page 126: Word Review

Synonyms

1. be back	5. arrive
2. begin	6. fall
3. immediately	7. friendly
4. about	8. soon

Antonyms

1. dangerous	5. save
2. far	6. come from
3. hard	7. low
4. out	8. a little

7. Sports and Fun

Page 130: A House at the Shore

III. Sentence Completion

1. next	5. start
2. shore	6. wonderful
3. vacation	7. then
4. rent	8. lie on

IV. Paragraph Completion

1. vacation	5. ocean
2. starts	6. lie on
3. rent	7. next
4. shore	8. wonderful

Page 133: A Picnic

III. Sentence Completion

1. shall	5. beautiful
2. great	6. about
3. far	7. kids
4. let's	8. bring

IV. Word Order

1. Let's go to the park.
2. Is it a nice place?
3. I'll make some sandwiches.
4. The kids will love it.

Page 136: I'm Going Skiing

III. Sentence Completion

1. fun	5. too
2. terrific	6. dangerous
3. maybe	7. worries
4. have got	8. careful

IV. Paragraph Completion

1. have got	5. dangerous
2. maybe	6. too
3. fun	7. worry
4. serious	8. careful

Page 139: A Soccer Game

III. Sentence Completion

1. team	5. hope
2. begin	6. later
3. best	7. busy
4. soccer	8. win

IV. Word Order

1. I'm going to play soccer.
2. Are you a good soccer player?
3. What time does the game begin?
4. I hope your team wins.

Page 143: Peace and Quiet

III. Sentence Completion

1. build	5. enjoy	9. carpenter	13. relax
2. pack	6. often	10. country	14. spend
3. leave	7. repair	11. excellent	15. sells
4. feeling	8. quiet	12. peace	16. real estate

Page 146: No Children This Year

III. Sentence Completion

1. together
2. lonely
3. couple
4. without
5. away from
6. usually
7. both
8. few
9. woods
10. stay up
11. fresh
12. noise
13. heat
14. long
15. forget
16. be able

Page 147: Word Review

Synonyms

1. fun
2. relax
3. busy
4. repair
5. often
6. spend
7. enjoys
8. wonderful

Antonyms

1. win
2. beautiful
3. north
4. best
5. now
6. noise
7. heat
8. leave

8. Schools and Children

Page 151: Is English Difficult?

III. Sentence Completion

1. a lot
2. blocks
3. difficult
4. learning
5. fun
6. have to
7. kind
8. practicing

IV. Paragraph Completion

1. learn
2. blocks
3. difficult
4. has to
5. kind
6. fun
7. practices
8. a lot of

Page 154: A Lazy Boy

III. Sentence Completion

1. surprise
2. angry
3. well
4. smart
5. maybe
6. afraid
7. so
8. lazy

IV. Word Order

1. I'm very angry at my son.
2. He's not doing well in school.
3. Jim is a smart boy.
4. Did you talk to his teachers?

Page 157: Not So Young

III. Sentence Completion

1. how
2. young
3. true
4. graduate
5. get married
6. next
7. so
8. remember

IV. Paragraph Completion

1. young
2. got married
3. graduating
4. so
5. how
6. next
7. remembers
8. true

Page 160: What's a Grant?

III. Sentence Completion

1. must
2. expensive
3. grant
4. great
5. loan
6. government
7. difference
8. pay back

IV. Word Order

1. My daughter is going to college.
2. That's great, but it must be expensive.
3. The government is giving her money.
4. You have to pay back a loan.

Page 164: Long Hours and Hard Work

III. Sentence Completion

1. close	5. understand	9. sells	13. sound
2. owns	6. take care of	10. almost	14. listening to
3. outside	7. too	11. changes	15. housework
4. hard	8. never	12. hear	16. pronounce

Page 167: Excellent Students

III. Sentence Completion

1. worries	5. ideas	9. excellent	13. feelings
2. different	6. seems	10. pay attention	14. ways
3. business	7. half	11. second	15. best
4. facts	8. respect	12. lessons	16. engineers

Page 168: Word Review

Synonyms

1. be expensive	5. sound
2. angry	6. grant
3. problem	7. half
4. maybe	8. pronounce

Antonyms

1. smart	5. child
2. more	6. excellent
3. well	7. take
4. graduate	8. change

Word List

The words used in the sentence and paragraph completion exercises and the word review exercises are listed below.

A

(be) able 146
about (adverb) 73,118, 126,133
about (preposition) 20
afraid (of) 76,104,154
after 42
again 7,67
age 49
all right 62,63
almost 101,122,164
alone 20
a lot 7,21,38,151
a lot of 73,151
already 101
also 20,21,80,125
always 17,67
angry 41,104,154,168
another 38,94
answer 62,80,125
any 13
anything 52
appetite 83
apply 73
appointment 31
arrive 125,126
at night 10
awake 10
away from 146

B

(be) back 115,126
bad 42
baked 13
bakery 52

beach 125
beautiful 133,147
because 20
begin 101,118,126,139
beginning (noun) 46,63
belong 41
best 62,139,147,167
better 28,42
big 63
bill 38
birthday 49
block 151
born 41
both 101,146
brave 58
briefcase 55
bring 133
build 143
business 167
busy 7,80,139,147
buy 20,63,73,115

C

calorie 17
can 4,21
careful 17,136
carpenter 143
cash 73
cashier 94
change (noun) 164
change (verb) 62,112,168
child 168
children 63
clean 67
close (verb) 101,164

closet 91
clothes 20
cold 28
collect 41
collection 41
come from 126
comfortable 76
compare 41
completely 104
computer 58
cook 4
cooler 109
correct 104
cost 73,125
count 101
country 143
couple 146
cousin 49
cry 122

D

dangerous 118,126,136
daughter 52
dear 91
degree 112
department store 38,125
diet 17
difference 160
different 17,21,55,167
difficult 83,151
dinner 4,21
dirty 67,84
dream 122
drive 73
due 46

E

early   17,97
easy   84,94
eat out   83
either   80
else   52
engineer   167
enjoy   143,147
especially   101
every   28,58,125
excellent   80,84,143,
    167,168
expensive   38,160,168

F

fact   167
fair   80
fall   126
far   118,126,133
fast   17,21
favorite   17,62,112
feel   28,58
feeling (noun)   143,167
fever   31
few   20,21,146
fight   20,104
file   80
find   94
finish   38,42
first   41
fish   13
fix   80
fly   76
foolish   76,84
forget   104,105,146
fresh   146
friend   105
friendly   20,122,126
full (of)   91
fun   80,136,147,151
future   83,84

G

get (arrive)   52
get (become)   58
get (obtain)   13,55,91
get back   52
get married   125,157
get up   97,105
glad   88,105
go back   122

God   28
good   4
go out   38
government   160
graduate,   38,157,168
grant   160,168
great   21,46,133,160
grocery   122

H

half   167,168
handsome   83,84
hanger   70
happy   42
hard   42,62,126,164
hate   97,105,109,118
have got   136
have to, has
    to   38,42,73,97,122,151
hear   25,164
heat   146,147
heavy   7,21,83,115
herself   41
hit   104
hobby   41
hope (noun)   83
hope (verb)   28,62,139
hot   21
housework   164
how   49,118,157
how about   13,55
however   80,84,104
how much   88
hurt   34,80

I

ideas   167
if   7,122
immediately   126
inch   62,118
in front of   67
in order   67
in style   91
insurance   58
interesting   58,94
interests   62

J

job   63
jog   58
joke   104

K

keep   10,94,105
key   7
kid (noun)   133
kid (verb)   104
kill   109
kind (adjective)   70,84,151
kind (noun)   94,105
kitchen   4
know about   41

L

large   63
last   38,42,58
late   17,25,42
later   31,139
laugh   104,105
lawyer   80
lazy   109,154
leaf, leaves   112
learn   101,151
leave   143,147
lesson   101,167
let   55,91
let's   133
lie on   130
like (preposition)   41
listen (to)   20,164
little   10,21,94,126
live   105
living room   17
loan   73,160
lonely   146
long   63,146
look   88
look for   31,94
low   126
lucky   97

M

magazine   62
mail   115
many   84
married   49,63
marry   38
maybe   76,136,154,168
mechanic   80
meeting   76
member   41
menu   13
mess   67